INTRODUCTION

As the British Royal Armoured Corps (RAC) approached the mid-1980s, is was becoming obvious to the Ministry of Defence (MoD), a department not noted for its swift appraisal of things, that the current situation in the Corps was basically unacceptable. Although some regiments had been equipped with the Challenger 1 – introduced with great fanfare as the saviour of the RAC – the reality wasn't quite as bright. The backbone of the UK Armoured Corps was still the 1960s-generation Chieftain – now in its Mk 10 and Mk 11 configurations – and Challenger 1. While Challenger 1 had the new Chobham armour, Hydrogas suspension and a new powerpack, internally the gun and its associated equipment were still very much of the Chieftain era. At the same time the potential enemy seemed to be advancing in leaps and bounds.

On top of that was the nightmare situation of maintaining logistics for two very different main battle tanks, that between them had very little in the way of commonality. All this time the UK had been trying to find a solution to the problem but to no avail. At this point the decision was taken that UK needed a brand-new tank. This was the easy decision. The rest would be mired in politics, and national pride. Many said buy off the shelf: two senior officers at Bovington were heard to say, 'We should stop messing about and buy Abrams.' This, it proved, would be a common theme for the next few years, with the German Leopard thrown in, as well as, for a while, the French Leclerc.

During this time frame, the Master-General of the Ordnance, Sir Dick Vincent, visited Vickers, and asked them to produce a proposal that would enable

The Chieftain in its final configuration as a Mk 11. Plans were laid for the Mk 12 and Mk 13 but were shelved. This tank and Challenger 1 constituted the British tank fleet, creating a logistical nightmare in keeping two vastly different tanks operational. (Rob Griffin)

A rank outsider, the French Leclerc. In itself it was a very good tank but fell foul of the British need for a four-man crew and the distrust of an automatic loader. (Joint Forces)

The replacement of the British tank fleet became something of an urgent requirement as it was operating both the Challenger 1 (seen here at Bovington) and the Chieftain that was still soldiering on. (Challenger Tank Appreciation Society)

The second main contender was the American M1 Abrams, again highly favoured in many quarters, but its stumbling block was its gas turbine engine, which, being too thirsty on fuel, did not fit in with British design requirements. (FAS)

the entire by-now geriatric Chieftain fleet to be replaced. The new tank was not to be so much a brand-new design but rather a further version of Challenger 1, like Challenger 1 Mk 3. This was in order to have an MBT fleet based on one vehicle, with all the early Challengers being brought up to a new build standard. That's about as far as that proposal ever got. The new tank emerged years later and was named, with a stroke of sheer genius by the MoD, Challenger! This soon changed to Challenger 2. It first came into the hands of the RAC regiments during 1998.

What of the period from that first tentative request to the vehicle actually arriving with the end-users? Well, it was not simply a case of saying to Vickers, 'Build us a new tank' and it all happened from there. Far from it. Vickers had formalized the concept of Challenger 2 and sent their ideas to the MoD. While parts of the proposal were acceptable, others were not – nothing unusual in a project of such magnitude. The original design was thus rejected by the MoD. Nearly 10 per cent of the design had to be reworked. With the MoD the resulting final version can often look nothing like the designers originally envisage. There were many outside issues that had to be taken into account, such as the changing political landscape, especially in Russia where it was hoped there might be a reduction in tensions. There was, of course, the ongoing battle with the Treasury. And lastly, the thought that perhaps the use of tanks was over: a familiar cry still heard today.

So, what were the available proposals that the government had to ponder over? The requirement also stated that the Chieftain replacement needed to be in the field by 1993. To make things really simple for the MoD, there were nine contenders for the new vehicle. First in the line-up was, believe it or not, Chieftain. This was to be produced in an improved form, but would really have necessitated a complete redesign – virtually a new tank. It could not, however, meet the necessary standard without large expenditure, so it was never really going to be in the running as a serious contender. What appeared to be a cheap and simple

solution was to discard the Chieftain and replace one for one with a Challenger 1, built to current standards. However, this really did not help as it was still hanging on to old technology. Challenger 1 was also on offer, with all the proposed upgrades. Also on the table was Challenger 1 with a smoothbore gun, although whose smoothbore gun was to be used was not mentioned: the UK was not enthusiastic about smoothbores at the time. Also on the smoothbore trail came Challenger 2. Next up were the foreign competitors, namely the German Leopard 2 and the United States M1 Abrams. Both contenders were examined in great depth as to their suitability. But in the background were rumblings of national pride, that the new tank must be British and built in Britain.

The Leopard 2 was highly favoured in many armoured circles, due to its high mobility and ease of maintenance. Chieftain's poorer mobility and the time – eight hours or longer – to change a powerpack, compared to Leopard's one hour, was a major consideration. But Leopard 2's big weakness was that the block-shaped turret offered no more protection than the Stillbrew add-on armour for Chieftain did. It was felt that to try and add on Chobham or a successor would not be feasible. One British-viewed design fault was having the majority of the ammunition above the turret ring in the large turret bustle. It was also felt that the NBC system was unsophisticated. The Germans did not help matters by refusing to disclose the armour protection that different turret versions had: potential purchasers need to know this sort of data.

Next up was the American Abrams M1A1. Overall, it was judged as ticking most boxes but, as always, there are inevitably faults or one country's design is incompatible with another's. For the M1 it was felt that the commander's station was uncomfortable and not very ergonomic. The one issue that caused much discussion and controversy was the fitting of the 1,500 gas turbine, an extremely thirsty beast. In the earlier versions of the M1 the engine had to be run constantly to provide electrical power. Whereas, in the UK, tanks fitted with an auxiliary engine could be run while the main engine was switched off, thus saving fuel and reducing the infrared signature generated by an engine constantly running, It was mooted to replace this with a diesel for UK use but this was ruled out as too expensive, with the added proviso that it might not work at all. Armour protection for the M1 was provided by depleted uranium, which, it was estimated, provided better protection than the proposed Dorchester armour – the latest version of Chobham armour – designated for Challenger 2. It was surmised that it would provide better protection against armour-piercing rounds but was not so good against rounds such as HEAT or HESH, whereas Dorchester

One of the tanks that Vickers produced as a private venture was the Vickers Valiant. Although it never sold, much of the data gathered from it went into the next Vickers tank and from there to what would be known as Challenger 2. (Military-Today.com)

The next Vickers private-venture tank was the Vickers Mk 7/2, again never sold and only one built. It was very fast with the armour, even with the designated add-on packs, just less than the current Challenger 2. A lot of its design features were updated and incorporated into Challenger 2. (Military-Today.com)

was. It came down to the fact that the real big mark against the M1 was the gas turbine. It should be remembered that the tank would have been modified to suit UK requirements, so these really are the major issues that had to be overcome. If the Challenger 2 project had not come to fruition then the M1A1 is the tank that the UK would have purchased.

One other contender was ruled out early on, due to the fact it used a three-man crew. This was the French Leclerc, a novel tank in its own right but the three-man crew went against UK doctrine: trials had shown that the degrading effects of a three-man crew during operations were not sustainable.

Vickers were quickly emerging as the most likely winners of the contract. The design they had formulated was based on their experience with Challenger 1 but also with their private ventures. Vickers were known to come up with ideas and rather than wait for a government decision, would go ahead and build the vehicle anyway. Although a gamble, over the years it had proved quite successful strategy. The one private-venture tank that helped shaped Challenger 2's design was the Valiant – another unoriginal name, as one had been

built during the Second World War that now resides in the Tank Museum. The Valiant – 'mark 2' – was developed in the late 1970s as a private venture. Although this is the name it is most often referred to, in Vickers' parlance it is the Vickers Mk 4. The prototype was completed in 1979. Vickers were pursuing their goal of private production to swell their numbers of foreign customers, those who wanted a modern tank but could not afford the current in-service vehicles. However, there were problems with the project and eventually it was halted with no sales being made.

Vickers decided to make use of the newly developed Chobham armour, as it weighed a lot less than conventional armour but still gave the protection. The Mk 4 was built with an aluminium hull. However, the turret was built in steel thus providing a light and fast tank. If required, add-on armour packs could be fitted to increase protection; however, a major flaw soon appeared when it was found that the aluminium hull was not up to the stresses imposed by the steel turret. The Valiant had what was called a universal turret in that it could mount the current UK 120mm rifled gun, the German 120mm smoothbore or the French 120mm smoothbore. The fire-control system was the Centaur system developed by Marconi and also fitted into Chieftain 900, for the time a highly advanced system.

The second tank that is part of Challenger 2's lineage is the Vickers Mk 7/2. This was a development of the Vickers Mk 7 which mated the new universal turret with the hull of the Valiant. This was not a success, again due to top-weight issues. So, the Mk 7/2 was born. The solution was to take the universal turret and fit it onto the hull of the German Leopard 2, giving it a solid, dependable and proven hull. The result was a 54.6-ton tank powered by a German 1,500hp 47.6-litre MTU MB 873 Ka-501 engine from the Leopard 2A4. Vickers built a single prototype in 1985 and the result was a rather good-looking tank that could be armed with either the 120mm GIAT and Rheinmetall smoothbore or the British L11A5. The fitted Marconi Centaur fire control system was state of the art, as were its sights and thermal imager. The British Army actually looked at this vehicle, but the problem with the Vickers' private venture tanks was that their armour protection was not up to specification. Valiant, even with its add-on Chobham armour, had less protection than Challenger 1. Obviously, Vickers were disappointed but they had learned a lot from these two tanks and these lessons were used in the development of the Challenger 2.

The UK seemed to be heading for a pure UK-designed and built tank. The Germans had offered to redesign and improve the areas that fell short of the UK requirements. However, this was rejected by Prime Minister Margaret Thatcher, who clearly wanted a UK tank and is reputed to have asked, 'Can we not design a tank of our own?' Thus, the ball was well and truly back in Vickers's court. After further arguments on cost and numbers and dates into service, on the 20 December

1988 Secretary of Defence George Younger announced in Parliament that Vickers had won the contract to produce the new tank. This would be spread over a two-year period to allow Vickers to prove that they could actually do what they said, and to this end funds were procured to manufacture nine prototypes. Several issues still were being thrashed out. One was the proposal for a 1,500hp diesel powerpack instead of the 1,200hp version in Challenger 1. This died a death thanks to the Treasury, as did a lot of work on the capability to allow the commander to fight the tank at night using the proposed panoramic thermal imaging sight. So, the 1,200hp pack from Challenger was to be retained, even though as a private venture Vickers modified a Challenger 1 using the 1,500hp euro pack, which was compact and for a tank engine extremely quiet, but again, those pulling the purse strings denied the funding. The other issue was the use of the 120mm smoothbore to allow commonality between the American, German and the UK models. The downside was the fact that to mount the smoothbore would require a major redesign of the turret, and again cost came into it. This issue would reappear again in Challenger 2's life.

This is a very concise introduction to the reasons why Challenger 2 evolved but is by no means the definitive version. Omitted are the major problems and the total halting of the production line due to the number of faults found during inspections of service vehicles at the depot at Ludgershall. This had a knock-on effect of leaving the first regiment slated to receive Challenger 2 with no tanks at all as they had returned their Chieftains. This was a bit embarrassing, but thankfully the Russians had their own issues at the time. Suffice to say that the problems were identified and action plans put in place to rectify the system so production could recommence.

A side view of Challenger 2 showing just how similar the hull is to its predecessor; however, that is where the resemblance ends. (Challenger Tank Appreciation Society)

Challenger 2 in Detail

Take a crew who served on Conqueror or Centurion and slot them into a Challenger 2 crew station and they would feel at home. The tank retains the normal British layout of three-man turret and driver. However, that's where the resemblance to Conqueror and Centurion ends, for although some items would appear familiar, the technology inside the tank has advanced beyond anything they could have dreamed of.

The Hull

At first glance the hull looks very much like its predecessor Challenger 1 and the very early versions did resemble it, but that's as far as it went, although, when Challenger 2 first appeared, it was said that it was just a new turret on the old hull, and in fact the commonality between the vehicles was quoted as being less than 15 per cent. The hull contains the driver's compartment in the front. The centre part is taken up by the fighting compartment. The rear, which is separated from the fighting compartment by a sealed bulkhead, contains all the automotive systems, powerpack – the engine and cooling systems integrated into one unit for ease of removal, although in Challenger 2 the concept has been taken further with the gearbox being part of the powerpack – plus the gearbox, auxiliary generator, final drives and the compressor for the crew temperature control system known as the CTCS. (Challenger 2 introduced a whole new list of abbreviations and acronyms to the tank world, and to listen to a talk on the vehicle is like listening to a new language.)

The actual hull is made up of welded steel plates, which are some of the thinnest parts of the tank. In the hull bottom are various access points and drain plugs for the various components. The hull top has the driver's location at the front in the centre. The location of the seat, driver's hatch and his periscope are designed so that like Chieftain and Challenger 1 the driver can drive sitting upright with his head out, or in a supine position with the hatch closed and using the periscope or, if fitted, a forward-looking camera. The periscope is provided with a wipe-wash system and can be replaced with the L41A1 driver's night-driving periscope, an image-intensifier sight for night-driving. This is a throwback to Challenger 1, the change from day to night taking only a few seconds.

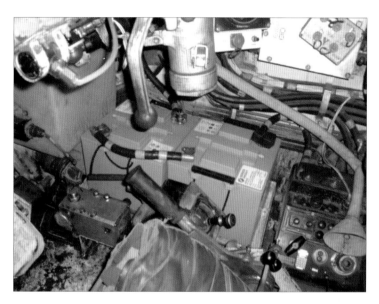

Inside the driver's cab. Showing the batteries to the right of the seat and the small stubby gear selector and one of the steering levers, this system for steering the tank is preferred by the British. (Rob Griffin)

However, in a chemical environment, this cannot be done as in those few seconds the integrity of the vehicle pressure sealing would be breached. To steer the tank the driver has two steering levers, still the favoured British approach. Also located in the cab are all the instruments needed to start and control the tank.

Moving back from the driver is the fighting compartment, reached from both sides of the hull and which carries all the

This shows just how cramped and compact the powerpack installation is on Challenger 2; amazingly, the euro pack fits into less space, is smaller, more powerful and gives 1,500bhp. (Rob Griffin)

fighting equipment and the turret. The fighting compartment is separated from the rear part of the hull by a fireproof bulkhead. Located in the rear compartment is the powerpack and the other components of the automotive side of the tank.

As noted earlier, the powerpack concept embraces the engine, cooling system and in Challenger 2 the gearbox. This design makes an assembly change much simpler and quicker. The engine in this case is the CV12CTA, a 12-cylinder Rolls-Royce engine in the C range and configured in the V layout. To the crew this is the main engine. Coupled to this is the David Brown TN54 gearbox, a fully automatic gearbox, which eases the strain on the driver. However, he has a selector in his cab that he can use to select ranges should he need to, very much like some set-ups in a manual car. To provide power when the tank is stationary

The powerpack concept: lifting all the main components out in one move makes for easier lifting and swifter changes, compared to Chieftain that could run to a day or more. (Rob Griffin)

The use of double-pin track is clearly seen here with soldiers from the Royal Tank Regiment battling the track; the end connectors and the rubber pads are visible here. (British Army RTR)

for any length of time is the auxiliary generator, known to crews as either the 'aux gen' or the 'genny'. This is a wonderful piece of equipment in that the main engine can be shut down and it will supply power for all the turret services, including that most loved piece of British kit, the boiling vessel. This almost legendary item allows the crew to cook their rations and boil water, all very easy these days as most rations are now 'boil in the bag' types with the days of tinned rations long gone. Tactically it allows the vehicle to remain undetected in a position for a long time without the heat, noise and exhaust from the main engine. Compare this to the earlier Abrams that had to keep the gas turbine running at all times, creating fuel consumption issues, among others. Abrams, however, does now have an auxiliary power unit, to give it is American name.

Also located in the rear hull are eight main fuel tanks providing 1,592 litres that are under armour. A further 410 litres can be carried in the external fuel tank. Unlike Challenger 1 and Chieftain that used a similar system of fuel bags, Challenger 2 has a system called Exposafe. While this helps prevent the fuel exploding or catching fire, it has a drawback: because of the space it occupies, it slows down refuelling time compared to its successors. Challenger 2 has built-in on-board defuel/refuel pump and can refuel itself from the two external drums.

The tank is supported on twelve modified (from those used on Challenger 1) Hydrogas suspension units, which each carry twin aluminium road wheels. The latest wheels have lightening holes in them to help prevent the build-up of mud between the wheels. They are fitted with the normal solid-rubber tyres, which soon shred in harsh conditions such as the British Army Training Area (BATUS) in Suffield, Canada. Whereas its predecessors used a single-pin track, a double-pin live track was selected for Challenger 2. This track has internal rubber bushes which tend to make the track curl when laid down off the tank, unlike the single pin which will lay flat. Originally there were problems with the track end connectors failing but this has now been rectified. One job that has been made easier for the crew is the use of a hydraulic track adjuster. In Challenger 2's predecessors, to tighten or slacken the track, a rather large ratchet spanner was used which might take two crewmembers jumping on its arm to move the adjusting nut. Now it is controlled from the driver's cab, and a hydraulic ram pushes or retracts the idler wheel (the one at the front of the tank) and either tightens or slackens the track. While 'track bashing' is still hard, physical work, this does make a great deal of difference and helps speed up the time taken in that thankless task.

Between the driver's compartment and the engine compartment is the fighting compartment. This fills the area and runs from side to side; over this is the turret, so all in all it is a large compartment. This is where the real business of Challenger 2 takes place.

The loader has a turntable floor to stand on which rotates with the turret, a vast improvement on the early Centurions where the hull floor was what the loader stood on: when the turret turned, he had to be quick so as not to get trapped. The turret is mounted on bearings that form the turret ring. The turret is traversed by means of an electric motor which meshes into the teeth cut into the turret ring. Electric rather than hydraulic is a standard British safety feature and was one of the downsides to the Abrams as it uses hydraulic motors – if penetrated the hydraulic fluid can ignite and make a bad situation worse. The Israelis discovered this and made big changes to their American-supplied tanks to negate this accident waiting to happen.

The crew layout in the turret follows normal British practice with the commander on the right side seated above the gunner. The loader/operator/teamaker/sandwich-maker is located on the left of the turret. Between them is Challenger's 120mm L30 rifled gun, which is capable of firing APDS (armour-piercing discarding sabot), APFSDS (armour-piercing fin-stabilized discarding sabot), HESH (High-Explosive Squash Head) and smoke rounds.

A quick explanation as to the nature of the ammunition. The APDS was derived from the various AP rounds in use during recent conflicts, developed to make use of the energy released on the propellant exploding in the breech. Simple physics shows that a smaller-diameter object will travel faster for the same amount of explosion than a full-size projectile. The

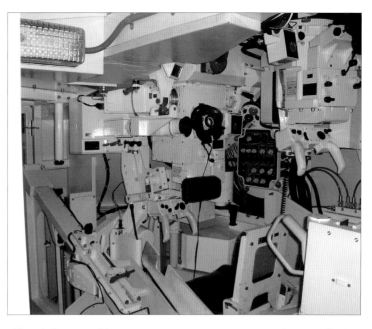

Although this is one of three troop gunnery trainers, it gives a very clear view of both the gunner's and loader's stations and also some of their controls. (Rob Griffin courtesy of RDG)

problem to overcome is that the bore is 120mm but you are looking at a much smaller diameter for your projectile. The solution is to encase it in a disposable shoe or sabot that is the same bore as the gun. Once the round leaves the barrel, the sabot falls off, allowing the solid core to travel at much higher velocity. It overcomes armour by sheer kinetic energy. The second round, APFSDS, is similar but during flight is stabilized by fins at the rear, rather like a giant dart. The HESH round is beloved by the British but when Challenger receives its upgrade, it may well be a thing of the past: Britain being the only nation to use it in NATO does not lead to commonality of supply. In essence, it is a slow-travelling

Taken a few years ago, this bunch of smiling RTR soldiers at the Castlemartin Range in Wales are doing a grand job of displaying the ammunition used on Challenger 2. From left: the practice round for the APFSDS round; next the propelling charges, white for HESH and orange for APFSDS; HESH practice round (all practice rounds are coloured Saxe-Coburg blue, the service rounds black for APFSDS and black with a yellow top for the HESH); and finally the belt of 7.62mm ammunition for the chain gun. (Courtesy RTR via Plain Military)

round compared to the armour-piercing one. It defeats armour by hitting the side of the target and, as it does, the side collapses, compressing the filling till it forms what in gunnery terms is called a 'cowpat'. The fuse in the base of the round then detonates, causing shock waves to bounce back and forth through the armour. Large 'scabs' are unleashed inside and fly around at high velocity causing untold damage and fearful casualties. The beauty of this round is that it will perform regardless of what range it is fired at, whereas armour-piercing rounds degrade after a certain distance. Finally, there is smoke which really does what it says on the packaging. Very few smoke rounds are actually carried – normally three rounds per tank – unless the requirement for a particular operation dictates otherwise: smoke screening is best left to the Royal Artillery.

RTR again, going through the ritual of bombing up. Practice rounds and bag charges are visible. The green flag denotes that all guns are clear (this is now indicated by lights). One might be forgiven for thinking this is BATUS judging by the camouflage scheme; however, it is the scheme used by the Land Warfare Centre at Warminster. (Courtesy RTR via Plain Military)

To ensure that all the rounds as discussed actually hit their targets, there has to be some type of sighting equipment for the gunner to use. For Challenger 2, when it was introduced for those used to Chieftain and Centurion style of gunnery, it was like stepping from an Apollo spaceship into the Starship Enterprise. The major change that increased the control of the gunner was that for the first time the gun was slaved to the sight electronically, instead of by manual linkage. In simple terms, with manual mechanical linkage, as the tank traversed across country, every movement of the stabilized gun would be transmitted into the gunner's sight. Thus, his view would be that of up and down images which, when trying to shoot while moving, made it a very much fire-and-hope system. With the current system the gunner has a steady view of the ground and the hit rate is so much better. The gunner has what amounts to three sighting systems to enable him to successfully carry out his task. The first is the gunner's primary sight (GPS). Looking at the outside of the turret, the GPS can be seen mounted in front of the large commander's sight. Also visible is the armoured sight cover, with protective hinged doors to the right to protect it when not in use. The head is provided with a wipe-and-wash system. The actual sight inside is much larger than anything a Chieftain or Challenger 1 gunner might recall. The days of the gunner just releasing his sight and dropping it in his lap to replace it with a new or night sight are gone. The sight is produced by the French company SAGEM with input from the British company Barr & Stroud, a name familiar to Chieftain and Challenger 1 gunners. The sight is gyroscopically stabilized. It also contains a laser rangefinder that is accurate to – or + 5m. It would be terrific eye strain for the gunner if he had to look through the x10 eyepiece all the time, so what is known as a unity window is provided. This is simply a x1 magnification window that allows him to sit back and have a wider field of view than through the main eyepiece.

The gunner is also provided with a secondary means of sighting and firing the gun should the main sight fail or be damaged. For this the Vickers L30 telescope is used, the range pattern inside used for

The armoured cover in the closed position protecting the gunner's primary sight head; a lever inside controls this cover. (Rob Griffin courtesy of KRH)

sighting being very similar to the one that was used on Challenger 1. It also doubles as the sight used to check the coincidence between the GPS and the bore, by means of the muzzle reference system (MRS). This simple device allows the gunner to check that his sight is aligned after every round fired; naturally he would not need to do this but the facility to do so is available. A light is shined from the light source located in the mantlet, and projected to the highly polished mirror that is normally hidden under the rubber shroud at the end of the barrel. Light is reflected back from this into the L30 telescope head and the gunner can adjust the sight alignment if necessary.

To control the gun and turret when using the power systems, the gunner has a unit mounted just near his lap known as the gunner's control handles, not unlike a games console. This design was apparently deliberate so that young crewmen would feel at home. Having visited the factory and spoken to the CEO, he says the truth is that after many trials to find the right ergonomic shape, this is what materialized. The unit allows the gunner to traverse and elevate the gun by means of a small thumb control. The turret can make a full revolution in twelve seconds. He also can fire the laser rangefinder from the unit and also fire the weapons from it. It also gives him something to hang onto and he is provided with a chest pad to prevent injury when travelling at speed. Below this is the hand traverse handle, used when the gun control equipment is not in use or broken. Located above the control handles is the hand elevating control, again for when it is not possible to use the power equipment. To his right is the gunner's control panel and from this he can control all the facilities he requires for his task. Next to it is the user control device which allows the gunner to access the Bowman radio menus without having to use the actual set itself. There is also a similar unit for the commander. Located just below this unit is the gunner's Bowman audio interface unit, which is where the gunner's crew helmet is connected and which will allow him to select various options on listening to the radio.

The final sighting system for the gunner is the thermal imaging sight. When this was introduced way back in the days of Chieftain Mk 11 and Challenger 1, it really was a game-changer, and made the 24-hour battlefield a reality. Prior to that tanks had to rely on either artillery or mortar illumination or in the case of Chieftain the use of either its IR sights (not much use) or white light (not very tactical). On Challenger 2 the thermal imaging sensor head is located in an armoured box which is known as the Barbette. This is unlike Challenger 1 where it was mounted on the turret side and which caused problems in alignment of gun, sights and the TI itself due to the offset. This has been overcome

The head of the gunner's auxiliary sight, used when the main sight is inoperable. (Rob Griffin courtesy of KRH)

This shows the MRS with the access cover replaced and in its normal operating position. (Rob Griffin courtesy of KRH)

This shows the mirror location under the shroud of the MRS that can be used by the gunner to accurately bore-sight the sight and gun after each shot if needed. Prior to this, the gunner would have to dismount and fit the bore sight into the barrel, not a good idea in combat. (Rob Griffin courtesy of KRH)

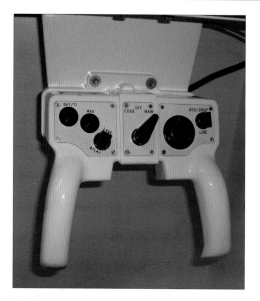

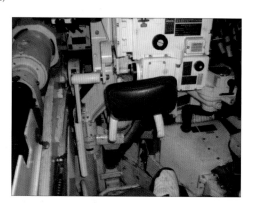

The view of the commander's station in the troop trainer; as near as possible the equipment replicates the service equipment. The whole system can accommodate three crew and allows troop fire control to be realistically practised. (Rob Griffin courtesy of RDG)

The famous gunner's control handle. When it first appeared, it generated a whole myth of its own, due to its resemblance to a games console; the truth is as described in the book. (Rob Griffin courtesy of Ultra Electronics)

Here the gunner's chest pad is visible in the centre of the picture; behind this is his primary sight. To the right can be seen the hand traverse handle, with the bulk of the L30 to the left. (Rob Griffin courtesy of RAC Gunnery School)

in Challenger 2 by mounting the Barbette directly above the 120mm gun. The thermal sight is often thought of as a night sight but as it detects heat sources, in can be used in daytime engagements as well and this is encouraged. You only have to see the thermal cameras in use on the many police programmes to see how heat sources give away the location of miscreants.

All this is controlled by a fire-control computer located on the turret floor directly below the commander. As noted earlier, the influence of the Vickers Mk 7/2 private-venture tank had input into the Challenger 2 design and this computer is a development of the one used on the Mk 7/2 for the Centaur fire-control system. The computer was built by Marconi and controls all the power systems needed for the gunnery on the tank. It does so much more but this is well beyond the scope of this account.

The commander's station is directly above the gunner. Access for the commander and the gunner is via the commander's cupola hatch. For the first time in a long while on a British tank the commander's cupola is not traversable. So, 360° viewing is achieved by the commander's primary sight itself being able to traverse the full 360°. For those who have served in any of

the previous tanks, to obtain that all-round vision the commander had to hand-traverse the cupola and at the same time try and contort his head to see out of it, a most uncomfortable and unsatisfactory system. The sight is the large box-shaped fitting forward of the commander's cupola. It is made by SFIM of France. The sight contains a laser rangefinder, but does not have a night-viewing facility. This is one of the items cut from the original design when it was requested that this facility be available to the commander. The sight is contained in an armoured box and when facing directly ahead is equipped with a wipe-and-wash system. The sight also gives the commander the choice of high or low magnification. The high is used for engaging targets or searching for likely enemy positions. The low allows a more relaxed viewing and also a larger sight picture, like the gunner's unity window, already mentioned.

Should the commander not wish to use the CPS, then he is equipped with eight periscopes located around the cupola rim. The commander's station has several duplicates of the gunner's controls, along with control panels particular to the commander's role. The commander has the facility to line the turret to the line of sight of his sight to speed up target acquisition. In simple terms, when the commander spots a likely target through low magnification, he can then swath high to confirm what it is. This is important so that blue-on-blue engagements are avoided but it also allows him to select the correct ammunition to be used. Once he is happy, he presses the align switch on his firing handle and releases it. This then causes the turret and sight to move till they are in alignment. The gunner's sight will switch to high-power magnification. All being well,

The commander's sight head for his primary sight. The protective shutters are in the closed position; this sight rotates 360° allowing the commander a good all-round view superior to that of its two predecessors. (Rob Griffin courtesy of KRH)

The meterological probe in its raised position. This will give the fire control computer weather information relevant to the tank's position only, as conditions down at the intended target may be very different. Note to the right the rubber-covered plug, where the amber rotary light is fitted; this is used during road marches. (Rob Griffin courtesy of KRH)

the aiming mark will appear in the gunner's sight, before the rest of the drills are then carried out to complete the engagement. Once the commander is satisfied that the gunner is laid on a correct target, he can if he wishes hunt for another target. This is what was known as the hunter/killer role. Another item that helps ensure that the first round fired is a hit is located on the turret roof. This is the Met probe. It can be either raised or if not required lowered into a recess in the turret roof. Its purpose is to provide local weather data – the weather conditions in the immediate vicinity of the tank – which are fed into the fire-control computer to make the final calculation more accurate. It does not and cannot predict the weather at the target.

The commander has a seat that can be lifted so he has his head out of the cupola. A hydraulic pump can raise it further if required. The cupola hatch can be left in the upright position, or partially closed in what is known as the umbrella position which gives space for manual viewing while providing overhead cover, and finally, fully closed down. Again, another change to British design is that the commander does not have a commander's machine gun, as in the Conqueror days and before. This has now been handed over to the loader as part of his duties, which does allow the commander to have one less thing to worry about.

The final turret member is the loader, a man of many tasks as we saw earlier. He is responsible for loading both the main armament and secondary armament,

keeping the ammunition fully stocked up and readily available, making food and drinks, manning the machine gun, looking after the radios, assisting the commander at times with map-reading and decoding the radio messages if required. He does, however, have more space to move than the other three crewmembers. The loader is responsible for ensuring that the correct nature of ammunition is loaded into the 120mm and for clearing any stoppages that may occur on the 7.62mm co-axial chain gun. Located around his space are the armoured charge bins that hold the bag charges for the main gun. These are below the turret ring level as is British practice. This helps protect the ammunition if the tank's armour is penetrated. The loader is responsible for tuning the Bowman radios and making any necessary adjustments. During lulls in firing he will ensure that ammunition stowed around the tank but not easily accessible is moved into the ready racks. Apart from being able to move around and stand head out of his loader's

This view looking down on the loader's side shows the charge bin and the turret floor; on the breech the moving part of the safety shield can be seen next to the breech. (Rob Griffin courtesy of RDG)

The original, unloved loader's GPMG mount, very reminiscent of the scarf mounting on First World War aircraft. It was eventually replaced by the simpler and easier-to-use pintle mount. (Rob Griffin courtesy of RMDC)

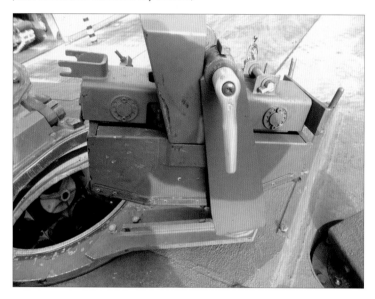

This is the improved and simpler pintle mount for the loader's 7.62mm GPMG. (Rob Griffin courtesy of RMDC)

Some of the stowage bins on top of the turret with their lids open. Compared to the Chieftain, Challenger 2 has a much cleaner and smother profile due to the way the stowage is organized. (Rob Griffin courtesy of KRH)

The remote weapon station fitting on Challenger 2; a similar version can also be fitted to both Trojan and Titan. The mount can carry the .50 Browning machine gun but in British service the 7.62mm GPMG is used. (QRH)

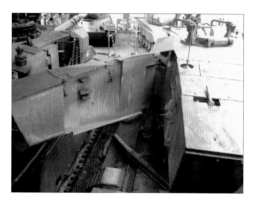

The side stowage bins hinge open to allow access to the panels behind. (Rob Griffin courtesy of KRH)

hatch, when closed down he is equipped with a No. 30 periscope. This is the same as fitted into Chieftain and Challenger 1. However, if the close-in weapon system is fitted, then this sight is removed.

A new task for the loader that has come about due to the design of Challenger 2 is that he now mans the turret-mounted machine gun which for a long time was the commander's remit. However, with a fixed commander's cupola this was not feasible, so rather than discard it, the loader ended up with the machine gun. The loader's hatch is mounted on a fully rotating ring so it was ideal for the gun to move to his location.

There have been two mounts for the 7.62mm GPMG. The first was a mount reminiscence of the gunners in First World War fighter planes, and it was universally disliked.   Later models of Challenger 2 had a simpler pintle-type mount fitted and this was gradually retrofitted to the earlier models. The stowage on Challenger 2 is more built-in than on Chieftain with its bins located all around the hull: on Challenger 2 the bins form part of the turret shape and can be swung out to allow access to the turret panels if required.

Weapons

The choice of the gun for Challenger 2 had to be a move from the L11A5 that was fitted to both Chieftain and Challenger 1. While there was nothing wrong with the gun, it had more

An amazing tank-firing picture that shows the burning gases and cloud at the barrel forced out by the action of the fume extractor; the fired round can be seen, clearly a HESH or practice round. (Trevor Gray)

What a squadron of night-firing Challenger 2s looks like: the sheer brightness is amazing and again demonstrates the latent power. (Courtesy RTR via Plain Military)

or less reached the end of its development life and could not be improved, notably in obtaining higher chamber pressures which in turn leads to higher muzzle velocities.

The choice was made to install the L30A1 120mm rifled gun in Challenger 2. In some aspects it follows the previous weapon in that it fires ammunition propelled by combustible charges. This means that unlike a brass/steel case, the whole case is consumed on firing with nothing to land back in the turret apart from a small-calibre igniting cartridge. This helps keep the turret clear and prevents the loader from having to dance over hot empty cases. Also, the charge can be placed below the turret ring in armour bins to help prevent an explosion if the tank is penetrated. The original bag charges had the explosive contained in a calico bag and if they got wet, they could not be fired. They are now contained in a more rigid casing made from Nitro Cellulose Kraft. Once the projectile and charge are loaded into the chamber and the breech is closed, they are fired by means of an electrically-ignited vent tube. This is nothing more than a small-calibre brass round that when initiated fires a shot of flame up a channel in the breech block which ignites the bag, which in turn will force the projectile down the bore of the gun. Ten of these rounds are held in a magazine located on the rear of the breech ring. Although a different design, the principle still follows that of the earlier L11 gun. Because of the use of a bagged charge, the gun has to handle obturation (the sealing of the breech by the rapid expansion of the brass/steel cartridge case). As the bag charge is consumed it cannot seal the breech, so another method was developed. In the L11 two machined obturator rings were placed into the breech mechanism, one in the front face of the breech block and one in the rear of the chamber. On firing, these were pressed together and formed a gas-tight seal. Due to an unfortunate accident in the early days of Chieftain when the gun was assembled with an obturator closed, various interlocks were introduced to prevent the breech closing if they were not fitted. An obturator sleeve protector was fitted to the top of the breech block and if the gas seal was failing, it caused a pin to protrude. The next time the protector

The loader's side. Although this is taken in the simulator, it shows all the main components, with the breech of the L30 dominating the space. On the white guard on the left of the L30 is an orange-tipped handle, one method of closing the breech. Next to it is the breech-opening handle. The 7.62mm chain gun can be seen just forward of this guard. (Rob Griffin courtesy of RDG)

This shot gives a good impression of what the ammunition looks like as well as some features on the turret. Most noticeable is the so-called bird table, the radio antennae base for the Bowman radio system. The orange cases are the charges in waterproof Nitro Cellulose Kraft; these are for the practice APFSDS rounds that can be seen on the turret. The smaller white bags are charges contained in calico for the practice HESH rounds also on the turret. Both practice rounds simulate the weight and feel of the service round. In the case of HESH there is no explosive, only concrete weight for the APFSDS that will perform as per the service round, except the long core is made of steel instead of tungsten. (QRH)

would be released and prevent loading of the gun as the two halves obstructed the mouth of the chamber.

For the L30 gun a system of obturation had to be found and a different type was employed. In the L30 the breech block is a vertically sliding one as was the L11, but this time the block is a split type in which both parts move. This is seen as a more efficient method, and to provide obturation a Crossley Neoprene pad-type obturator was introduced. The gun is located in the cradle which is fitted to the turret by means of trunnions with the armoured mantlet located on the forward part of it. The cradle contains the recoil system which is hydro-pneumatic. The breech is opened by the loader, initially by means of a breech-opening lever connected to the breech mechanism. Once the gun is loaded, he can close the breech in one of two ways: either by pulling on the breech-closing lever or he can pull the loader's guard to the rear. This method was first fitted to the Chieftain and was developed by S/Sgt Charlie Chase 4th/7th Royal Dragoon Guards and became known as the 'Chase mod'. On firing, the breech is opened automatically

ready for use; the vent tubes that initiate the change are loaded automatically. The end of the L30 has the muzzle reference sight mounted on the barrel top and is normally covered by a rubber shroud to help keep it clean.

The coaxial weapon is the L94A1 Hughes chain gun, which is an electrically driven 7.62mm machine gun. Due to the fact that the gun is operated electrically, any misfired rounds are ejected without the normal stoppage drill associated with the older GPMG. However, it does have its own problems and associated drills are designed to overcome these. It did suffer from lots of stoppages when first introduced into Challenger 2, eventually traced to poor-quality links that make up the ammunition belt. These were modified and the stoppage rate dropped.

The other weapon carried is the loader's 7.62mm GPMG. This weapon has been in service for nearly forty years, but is still the best there is. Capable of a high rate of fire, it was used on Chieftain and Challenger 1. On Challenger 2 it has been moved to the loader's side partly due to the fact his station is capable of 360° traverse while the commander's cupola is fixed. The weapon is used to lay down speculative fire and for close protection.

Other weapons are the twin banks of smoke grenades in groups of six, located either side of the turret on the forward edge. These are fired electrically by the commander to provide an instant emergency smokescreen, that will hopefully give the tank time to escape.

The crew also have personal weapons for when they are dismounted, usually a 9mm pistol for the commander and gunner and the carbine version of the SA80 rifle for the driver and loader, space permitting.

From past experience I am sure this will have the gunnery instructors jumping up and down, shouting and screaming. In reality the commander should of course be looking to his front to observe the fall of shot; however, it makes a brilliant picture and again shows the power of the L30 gun.
(Doug Bradbury, Challenger Tank Appreciation Society)

This is the barrel end of the 7.62mm chain gun as it protrudes through the mantlet. If you look closely at the image you will see that one of the prongs is round and appears hollow: this is where the spent cases are ejected, thus removing the requirement for having a container to collect the used brass cases in the turret as on previous tanks.
(Rob Griffin courtesy of KRH)

This RDG soldier is wearing the desert camouflage combat kit of the time. He is armed with the carbine version of the SA80 rifle, basically a cut-down version for easy carriage in armoured vehicles.
(Rob Griffin courtesy of RDG)

Challenger 2 Variants

It was hoped that in Challenger 2 the United Kingdom had a tank that would be an export winner and which would also be used as the basis for several variants of specialized armour. Sadly, although it was trialled and viewed by several countries, it just never seemed to cut the ice when it came to the actual purchase, bar one small order from the Omani army. Again, Vickers produced some versions that were heavily modified for specific areas but again no sales were forthcoming. This was very disappointing from the commercial view given that potential buyers tend to lean towards equipment that other nations have purchased. This left the United Kingdom as the major user of Challenger 2, which, while it might not have sold to the wider world, has served the armoured regiments proud and, with an upgrade being decided on as this book is being produced, will soldier on for many years yet.

The armoured forces of Oman had used the British Chieftain tank which had been in service with their armoured corps since the mid-1980s. Only numbering twenty-nine, it would be fair to say that with the best will in the world they were probably on their last legs. So, the Omanis cast around for a replacement tank. With its long-standing defence contracts and history with the United Kingdom, they viewed and saw Challenger 2 demonstrated and placed an order for it, making them the only export purchaser of the tank. However, before the tanks could be delivered, they had to be adapted to Omani requirements, as their version was not just an off-the-shelf purchase, which would have been simple. The order as placed called for eighteen tanks, two Driver Training Tanks (DTTs) and four Challenger Armoured Repair and Recovery Vehicles (CrARRVs) which had shown their mettle in the Gulf War. This order, which in the money of the time was worth around £140 million, was very welcome and was placed in 1993. It was followed up in 1997 with another twenty tanks, totalling £100 million.

The most obvious feature externally on the Omani Challenger is the fact that it uses the single-pin track of its predecessor Challenger 1. To support this purchase various training aids were also purchased including turret gunnery trainers. These are half-turret mock-ups that enable both

Two of the three troop turret trainers fitted at the RDG Gunnery Wing, Catterick. These allow three crews consisting of commanders and gunners to carry out realistic troop shoots with the troop leader practising his control of three tanks: a far cry from Centurion days when the targets were on wire traces drawn by electric motors and shot at with .22 rifles mounted on the turret. (Rob Griffin courtesy of RDG)

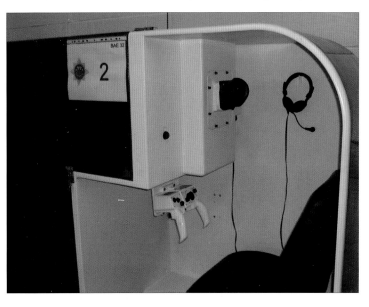

This little cubicle is the part-task trainer for the gunner. It allows him to practise electronically all the shooting skills he needs; it is in fact rather like a big expensive video game, but a great training aid and great fun. (Rob Griffin courtesy of RDG)

gunners and commanders to be trained in their various control skills. Also included were six part-task trainers: these look like a small cubicle with a representative of the gunner's primary sight that allows gunners

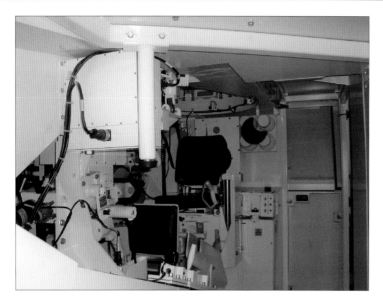

View from the front of the troop fire trainer showing the rear of the gunner's primary sight and the commander's station. (Rob Griffin courtesy of RDG)

A good overhead view of the loader's drill trainer (LDT). The coloured disc is located on the chain gun and if a stoppage occurs, this will give the loader an indication of the fault. The blue rounds in the stowage are specially designed replicas in size and weight of the service HESH round. Once loaded and the gun is fired, they will be extracted along with the charge and collected from the front of the trainer to be restowed. (Rob Griffin courtesy of RDG)

to practise their individual skills, great fun and rather like a large Xbox. There was also a loader's trainer included, which recreates the loader's side of the turret and allows the loader to practise loading and clearing misfires and stoppages and all other manner of problems that could happen in the real vehicle. All the faults can be inputted by the instructor. The gun in the trainer is loaded with special training rounds that represent the weight of actual service ammunition. As the gun is fired, it will recoil and a mechanism inside the barrel will draw the round and charge out which are then deposited into a container ready for use again. The gun recoils exactly as the full-size version which gives the loader realistic training at very little cost.

Some of the early tanks delivered had not had all the modifications that were being applied to the British fleet. They were subsequently brought up to standard with the cost being borne by Vickers. The major changes to the Omani fleet were dictated by the climate in which the tanks would be operating, namely high temperatures, and dust. The tank as produced would soon fall foul of these conditions so the changes made were as follows.

The first already noted was the choice of single-pin track and the use of Challenger 1 track. During Exercise Saif Sareea II not one Omani tank lost its tracks but several British Challengers managed to throw theirs. Whether this was due to the use of single-pin track opposed to the double pin is unclear. From the foregoing it is obvious that to cope with the higher operating temperatures any major improvement will be to the cooling system. Although the main engine and the auxiliary engine are more or less the same as the British version. the cooling system is modified to cope with the higher temperatures: the cooling air is drawn into the engine compartment through larger radiators then once it has helped cool the components, it is expelled through the three large louvres at the rear of the hull. These alone help distinguish the Omani from other Challenger 2s. It is said that the airflow is extremely strong compared to the normal Challenger 2 layout. This system also helps prevent dust being drawn into the main components when travelling at speed, as the tank creates its own mobile dust storm. To also help reduce dust the Omani Challengers are fitted with large, full-depth bazooka plates similar to those seen on Chieftain and Challenger 1. The air is drawn into the tank by means of three large fans that are powered by hydraulic pumps driven from the power take-off located on the gearbox.

A overhead view of the chain-gun mounting. The drill rounds denoted by the silver colour and indentations on their case are to the bottom left of the gun; also visible is the ready-round armoured charge bin, which allows the loader to practise all his loading and stoppage drills for the chain gun. (Rob Griffin courtesy of RDG)

Continues on page 50

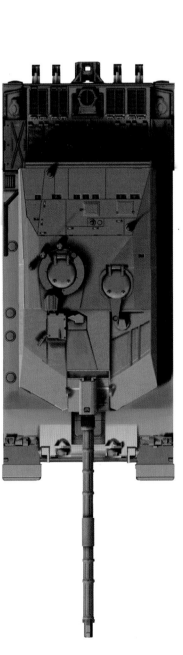

Basic

These four shots show what could be called a basic Challenger 2, as it is a bare-bones drawing, which enables the detail not to be cluttered up with the normal exercise add-ons so beloved by British tank crews. Notice the absence of the loader's GPMG and the approach fuel drums not fitted. This is quite often the norm to prevent damage; sometimes spare drums are cleaned out and one end cut off and covered with canvas to provide more stowage, to help cover Challenger 2's lack of storage. Of note for modellers, this tank is finished in the now-normal paint finish of overall matt green; it would seem the days of black/green camouflage are past. Also, I have heard modellers criticised at shows for the model not being the correct shade etc.; I would say ignore those comments, as the paint on a tank is affected by many factors, such as paint batch, weather, method of thinning and application. I saw one tank have the matt black camouflage applied but the paint was not mixed correctly; come the morning it had dried gloss. Pick an image of what you wish to build and stick to that. Although green is drab, there are lots of little things to add colour, as on the drawing the square for B Squadron call sign is yellow; add to that a number plate and other markings and the model comes to life.

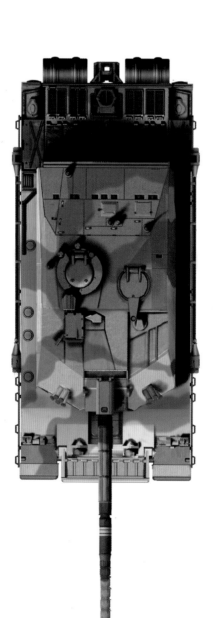

Land Warfare Centre

Although to those in the know, at first glance the response would be BATUS, due to the markings and camouflage scheme. Sadly, they would be wrong. This gives the modeller the chance to apply a different paint scheme to their rendering of Challenger 2. The vehicle is depicted wearing the colours of the Land Warfare Centre on Salisbury Plain; this organisation's vehicles have adopted the BATUS-style paint finish to distinguish them from units rotating through the Plain as they often are used as the enemy. Unusually, this tank has also adopted the BATUS method of having the call sign painted on the side skirts; it was also spotted carrying the glacis armour pack, although again it is not normal, and there are many reasons why. The tanks from Land Warfare and Tidworth garrison, besides carrying out their normal training duties, are often used to test out various items of equipment under development, which can involve many cold nights on the Plain to obtain the results. The call sign is applied to the turret rear and sides; again, if possible, use an actual image for your model, as there are different ways of painting, depending which unit is currently in-station. For example, if the Royal Tank Regiment were there, they would have their famous Chinese eyes on the turret. This tank is also very clean for Land Warfare, as their tanks and other vehicles are worked very hard.

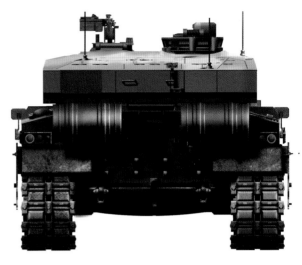

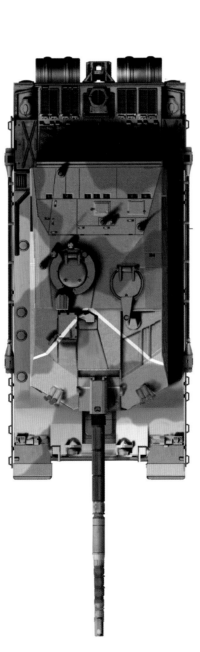

BATUS

This Challenger 2 is part of the fleet from BATUS in Canada, a vast training area used by UK forces that allows them to employ live fire and manoeuvre but under the strictest safety environment. The equipment at BATUS is probably the hardest worked in the Challenger fleet, with the tanks rotated back to UK usually every couple of years: working them hard is better for them than being left stored in hangars and only coming out occasionally for a couple of weeks. This vehicle would appear to have been freshly out of the winter maintenance period and probably only just taken over by the first unit of the new season. Each unit will apply the call signs that are applicable to the squadron participating. For how these are applied and coloured, refer to the Land Warfare image. Also painted onto the front of the skirt plates will be the vehicle BATUS ZAP number, unique to all vehicles and to each soldier taking part. It is a system that allows identification without giving names or call signs away, very important in the event of an incident. It has the loader's GPMG fitted and the meteorological mast in the upright position; it also has the approach fuel drums fitted. For modellers building a BATUS tank the most important feature is the two white lines at 45° from the commander's cupola. These painted lines are a very simple safety device, especially when closed down. If the commander can see a target appear between those lines, he will ask the safety staff travelling with the unit in their own vehicle (that have parts of the vehicle painted red, giving rise to the nickname 'Red Tops') permission to fire. If the safety staff are happy, the next thing is one loud bang as the target is engaged.

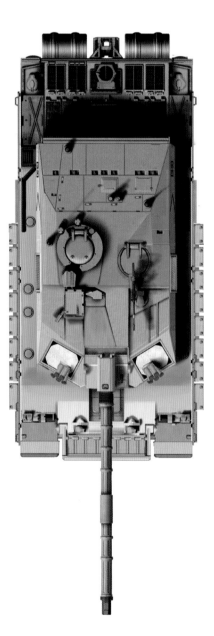

OP Telic Iraq

The four views of a Challenger 2 deployed to Iraq on one of the Telic operations show just how far the army has adapted since those early days of Gulf War 1 and Challenger 1. Even though this tank has most of the bells and whistles, there are more items that could be added; however, they are issued on a case by case basis, mostly due to the fact that kits were not produced for every Challenger, and will remain in-theatre to be used as and when. Items such as the bird table and other anti-IED devices are examples. Looking at this tank, it can be seen that it has the extended dust skirts hanging from the add-on side armour, a lesson learnt after the dusty conditions on exercise in Oman. Notice the slated recognition panels located on either side of the turret, added to try and improve recognition and avoid blue-on-blue engagements. It is fitted with the ERA armour glacis pack which was later upgraded to improve protection. Note the inverted black chevrons, a Coalition device to also help identify units: check your references for this. As this tank does not have the thermal cowls fitted over the exhausts, the telltale staining on the armour is present; again, the cowls were not fitted to all Challengers, so the best way of producing your model is to pick an image – there are thousands available but work to the one you select. In painting your model for Operation Telic – you could write books on the discussions on the use of the correct paint – there are several good accurate colours out there. Don't forget that your tank – unless you wish to display it in a just-painted setting – will be subject to wind, abrasion from the sand and general wear and tear, and very soon that beautiful showroom finish will be gone.

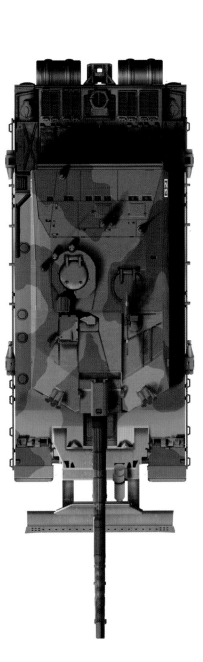

KFOR

The deployment of Challenger 2 to Kosovo was its first operational usage, although it was more as a deterrent than to actually bring its weapons to bear in anger. Much like its predecessor had achieved in Bosnia, the sight of a large lump of armour bearing down on your position does tend to make you think twice. Unusually, this tank has the dozer blade kit fitted (a bit like Marmite: either you love it or hate it). Way back in the Chieftain days, each squadron was issued a dozer blade, and unless needed they lived at the back of the vehicle hanger as no one liked having the blade fitted: very good for snow clearing though. The blade is traditionally fitted to the squadron second-in-command's tank, but it can be fitted to any tank. If you look at the lower glacis on a Challenger 2, you will see a round access plate: this is for feeding some of the power and hydraulic lines through from tank to blade, which produces a neater and safer arrangement than the Chieftain blade. The tank is painted in the then scheme of black and green, with the KFOR letters painted in white along the side skirts. Later deployments saw the side armour packs fitted. The call sign will be painted in the colours that the individual units would use, with white, black and yellow being normal. It has the loader's GPMG fitted and the meteorological mast is in the upright position. Despite its unpopularity, the blade could be very useful in digging shell scrapes for tank firing positions, removing damaged vehicles or debris from roads, and snow clearing. Vehicles deployed on Kosovo patrols were rarely seen covered in crew kit and camouflage nets, as they usually returned to the relative warmth of their bases at night.

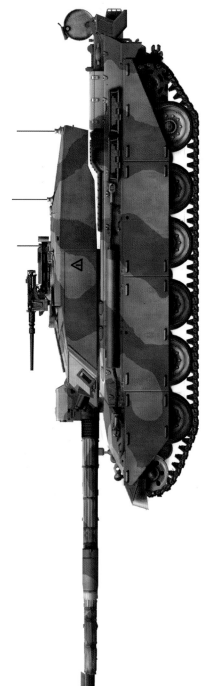

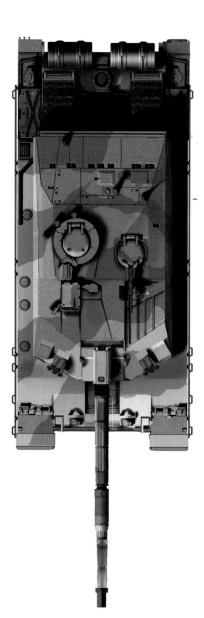

Oman

The Oman Challenger 2 makes a very interesting conversion from the normal tank. Oman, being the only other user of Challenger 2, requested some major differences to their version compared to the standard model. The first noticeable change is to the track, as the Omanis have opted for the single-pin track and sprockets from the Challenger 1. They have also replaced the loader's 7.2mm GPMG with the tried and tested Browning .50 heavy machine gun that has far more hitting power than the GPMG. Due to the extreme temperatures that the tank is expected to operate in, they have installed a more efficient cooling system, which has resulted in the very different rear of the tank: instead of the normal flat plate with all the tools on it, the Omani version has a large grill taking up the whole of the rear hull plate. This means that all the items fitted to the rear plate have now moved to the sides of the tank, and because of this the approach march fuel drums are located on the hull rear top, as is the travel lock for the 120mm; the rear decks are also laid out differently. Oman has tried several camouflage schemes including this one in the drawing. Again, check your references and decide what you are going to model.

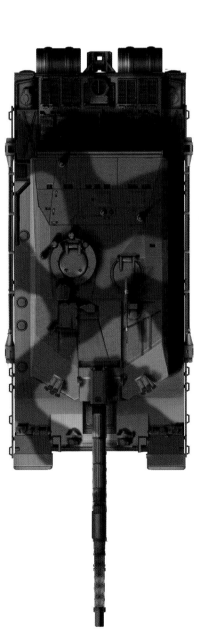

BAOR

When Challenger 2 arrived in what was then the British Army of the Rhine (BAOR), it was indeed a game changer, a welcome addition to the armoured regiments. The BAOR tanks followed the normal upgrades with the most noticeable being the removal of the unloved scarf-type mounting for the loader's GPMG and its replacement by a simple pintle mounting, as shown in the drawing. At the time of its introduction the paint scheme for the BAOR was still the green/black finish. Once tanks were deployed to Iraq, and spare parts were painted plain green, then the idea of two-colour camouflage seemed to drop out of favour; also, it was cheaper to only have one colour. For modellers painting this scheme, there is no real laid-down pattern as it was originally left to crews to carry out painting the tanks. But as health and safety moves into the forces, this does not happen anymore and, having painted a few in my time, it's probably a good idea. The tank in the drawing has the normal call sign painted on. Other markings are best gleaned from publications and photos of real vehicles: items such as convoy markings on the rear, registration numbers and tactical signs, and of course, for the BAOR the Union flag on front and rear wings.

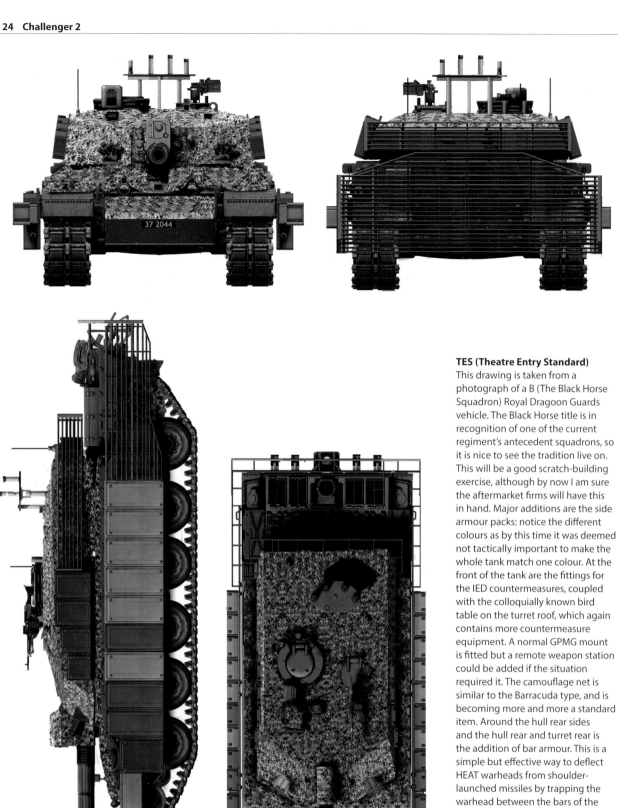

TES (Theatre Entry Standard)
This drawing is taken from a photograph of a B (The Black Horse Squadron) Royal Dragoon Guards vehicle. The Black Horse title is in recognition of one of the current regiment's antecedent squadrons, so it is nice to see the tradition live on. This will be a good scratch-building exercise, although by now I am sure the aftermarket firms will have this in hand. Major additions are the side armour packs: notice the different colours as by this time it was deemed not tactically important to make the whole tank match one colour. At the front of the tank are the fittings for the IED countermeasures, coupled with the colloquially known bird table on the turret roof, which again contains more countermeasure equipment. A normal GPMG mount is fitted but a remote weapon station could be added if the situation required it. The camouflage net is similar to the Barracuda type, and is becoming more and more a standard item. Around the hull rear sides and the hull rear and turret rear is the addition of bar armour. This is a simple but effective way to deflect HEAT warheads from shoulder-launched missiles by trapping the warhead between the bars of the armour. Finally, there are add-on armour packs either side of the turret. This is a full-on conversion and something out of the ordinary.

CHALLENGER 2
21st Queen's Royal Lancers, Operation Telic, Iraq
1/35 Scale
Steve Abbey

Inside the stout cardboard box, Tamiya have supplied five sprues moulded in light-tan plastic holding 345 parts, as well as another one in clear plastic holding 17 parts. There is also a sheet of thin white plastic card for the turret front CIPs plus a small clear sheet for the commander's cupola periscopes. Nuts and bolts, a length of twine for the tow cable and thin wire for the cable reel on the rear turret as well as the usual poly caps to the wheels in place are also present. A well-drawn 16-page instruction manual and decal sheet portraying three Challenger 2s from the Royal Scots Guards (Carabiniers and Greys) and the 7th Armoured Brigade (Operation Telic in Iraq during Spring 2003), complete the package. To create something different, it was decided to model a vehicle without the usual white CIP panels. To this end the 21st Queen's Royal Lancers during August 2004 was chosen from Star Decals' sheet 35-C1099 Operation Telic Challenger 2 part 4. Tamiya etched sheet (No. 35277), which comprises 8 different mesh screens, was used to enhance the engine decking.

Construction started with the lower hull, with all the road wheels glued together and located with the poly caps supplied. So as to limit any damage, the sponson supports were left off until further on in the build.

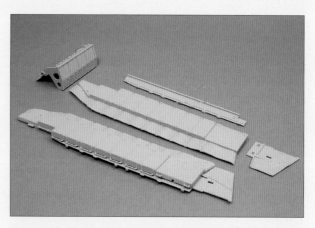

While the assembled parts were put aside to dry, work progressed with the reactive front armour and Chobham side skirts.

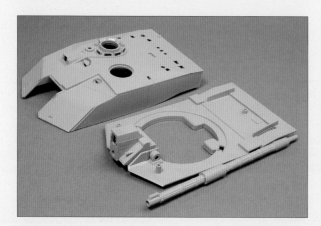

Hull and turret parts were then put together. The Tamiya etched grills fixed in place with a few drops of Cyanoacrylate Adhesive (CA). When dry, all sub-assemblies were sprayed with Halfords Grey Acrylic Primer.

To limit the potential 'see-through' around the rear of the skirts, plastic card inserts were cut to size and fitted above the drive wheels and visible part of the overhang. Any gaps were filled and sanded smooth.

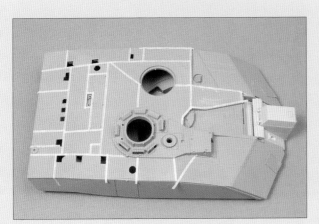

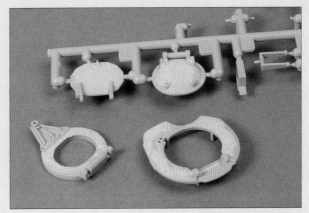

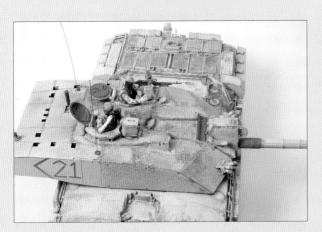

With the hull and turret parts put together, the Tamiya etched grills were fixed in place with a few drops of Cyanoacrylate Adhesive (CA). When dry, all sub-assemblies were sprayed with Halfords grey acrylic primer. Although Tamiya have produced a great kit, its main shortcoming is the lack of the anti-slip texture on most of the Challenger's upper hull and turret surfaces. This is easily rectified using Hull Tex, which is a two-part system from VMS. Areas to have a textured surface were brush painted with Hull Tex Cement. Then the Hull Tex Texture puffer bottle was used to coat the surface, with any excess tapped off and replaced in the bottle for future use.

After removing the masking tape, Tamiya XF-67 NATO Green was brush-painted into the resulting rough surfaces to form a tough finish. Detail on the side armour was enhanced by pre-painting with Lifecolor UA628 Mahogany Stain. AK Interactive AK4034 Light Stone was then airbrushed over the model. A watered-down wash of this colour was used on the rubber mudguards and tyres after they were painted Lifecolor UA-734 Worn Black. Several replacement panels were picked out with a lightened version of the Light Stone. To aid adhesion, areas to receive decals were painted with AK Interactive Gloss varnish. These went on without any problems. A fine sanding stick was used to rub away the top colour, where crew members had moved over the Chally and exposed the underlying paint.

Any overzealous paint removal was retouched with more NATO Green. The model was weathered using AK Interactive AK2019 Engine Oil – particularly over the engine grilles, AK2073 Panel liner for Sand & Desert Camouflage – over the bolt heads and main gun sleeve, and Lifecolor UA 263 Grease Effects-around the filler caps. Aerials were made from bristles cut from a broom. To protect the paint surfaces, the completed model was sprayed with a matt coat using Tamiya TS-80 Flat Clear. Finally, to generate a dusty appearance, Tamiya XF-57 Buff was sprayed in mist coats around the model, concentrating mainly around the sides and rear.

CHALLENGER 2
King's Royal Hussars (KRH), Salisbury Plain 2018
1/72 Scale
Timothy Neate

This model is based on a King's Royal Hussars (KRH) Challenger 2 circa 2018 on exercise on Salisbury Plain. It has the attachment points for the Dorchester Level 2F add-on armour, which are prominent features on the turret sides. Two manufacturers produce 1/72 scale injection moulded plastic Challenger 2, Dragon released their first example in 2004 with Trumpeter following in 2006. Both kits have issues, but after comparing the kits with my references the Dragon Challenger 2 had better detail and looked easier to correct.

The Dragon turret has a more accurately shaped front, although the loader's side had to be lowered to make it the same height as the commander's side. The rear of the turret was re-shaped by cutting across the turret roof around the cupola and down the sides following the panel lines. A new turret rear was produced from plastic card with the help of a set of scaled drawings. The panel lines were re-scribed and new cut-outs made for the storage bins' catches and antennae. Another plastic card layer was added beneath the cut-outs with bin catches positioned in each recess. False floors were made from black plastic card for the crew figures to sit on. The main gun mantlet was taken from the Trumpeter kit because it was a better shape than the one provided in the Dragon kit.

The commander's cupola was rebuilt and improved with new periscopes and hatch cover details. The commander's large panoramic sight was built from plastic card with open doors as were all other sights indicating a fully active vehicle. All turret optics were improved with the addition of wipers. The slimmer Bowman antennae mounts and GPS stud antenna were made and added to the turret roof.

A new chain gun barrel and Met probe was made. A new loader's cupola and machine-gun mount was built with a CMSC white metal GPMG fitted. Plastic tubing was used to make the turret side extra armour mounting points.

The driver's position was re-detailed with new periscope, handle and catches. A new trim vane and extra armour plate was built for the glacis plate with the addition of light fittings and fire extinguishers with mirror stalks made from metal rod. Thinner mudflaps were attached to the front track guards with the addition of riveting detail. The hull fire extinguisher pulls were moved back in line with the large panel line across the glacis plate.

The loader's side of the turret was lowered to make it the same height as the commander's side with Milliput used to blend in.

New engine deck handles were made from copper wire and engine deck prop from plastic rod. The gun barrel clamp was refined and detailed. The engine deck rubber bumper was detailed and the holes drilled out.

The air intake for the crew temperature control system was rebuilt and fixed to the rear hull plate. Resin oil drums replace the kit parts with mounting brackets and strapping made from plastic card. The ratchet strap handles came from the Extra Tech Challenger II etch sheet EXV72079.

The rear of the turret was re-shaped by cutting across the turret roof around the cupola and down the sides following the panel lines.

The new side skirts were
made from thin plastic card
with the addition of camouflage loops
and bolt heads. Copper wire tow cables replaced
the vinyl kit parts with new cable ends and securing catches.
I made a disc template to drill the 15 holes in each road wheel to
represent the latter design of wheel. Revell Leopard 2 link and length track was
used in preference to the vinyl type supplied in the kit. The hull rear was re-detailed with
mudflaps, light units, towing eyes, spare track link holders and the tow-bar equipment
which came from a Revell Challenger 1 kit. The double jerry can holders were shaped from brass rod and secured with superglue. The infantry
telephone and first aid box were built from plastic card and positioned next to the jerry can's holder. Catches were added to the toolboxes and the
crowbar added to the righthand side of the engine deck. Two more accurately made exhausts, along with the rear fuel filler caps and guards, were
re-positioned correctly on the hull rear.

The whole model was primed with Halfords Grey Primer before airbrushing the camouflage scheme using Vallejo Model Air US Interior Yellow 71.107
and Medium Olive 71.092. Individual details and equipment were painted in with a brush and homemade decals were applied (VRN, Callsigns and
Convoy marking). Some limited highlighting and shading was added to prominent details. Johnson's Klear was applied to protect the acrylic paint
from a dust wash of 90 percent white spirit to 10 percent paint mix of Humbrol No. 72 (60%) and white (40%). A textured mud effect was applied to
the lower hull using Plaster of Paris and No. 72 and white paint mix. Areas needing higher concentrations of dust were dry brushed using the same
mix of No. 72 and white. Winsor & Newton Liquin drying medium was added to the No. 72 wash and applied carefully to increase the dust effect.
Darker browns were used to depict wet mud, fuel spills and wear. Finally, a dark brown pin wash was applied around all details and panel lines.

The hull was corrected by removing about 1.5mm from behind the engine deck rubber bumper and cutting out the engine deck and moving it forward. The exhausts, rear fuel caps and guard were removed and the toolbox location holes filled. The location holes on the hull sides were also filled and the detail and side skirts carefully removed. Some of the smaller removed details were saved and re-positioned back on the model.

The commander's large panoramic sight was built from plastic card with open doors as were all other sights to portray a fully active vehicle. All turret optics were improved with the addition of wipers. The TOGS door was opened up and scratch-built TOGS equipment was painted and mounted inside.

CHALLENGER 2
4th Troop, 4th Squadron, 2nd Royal Tank Regiment, Operation Telic, Iraq 2003
1/35 Scale
Brian Richardson

This is the Tamiya kit 35274 that dates from 2004 and just as the full-size vehicle has improvements over the Challenger 1 so does this kit. It has been built to represent a tank from 'Flanders' 4th Troop, 4th (Falcon) Squadron, 2nd Royal Tank Regiment, Operation Telic, Iraq, 2003. It has had a few improvements with Meng nuts and bolts added and some photo-etch latches fitted to the toolboxes. Headlights were cabled with thin solder and missing details added with plastic card, wire, putty welds and Mr Surfacer 500 stippled over the hull and turret for the non-slip. Tarps and bed rolls were made from facial tissue and Millput. 16-gauge guitar wire was used for the aerials. Tamiya acrylics were mixed for the Desert Yellow, XF-52 Flat Earth used for the dust skirts.

The one-piece glueable vinyl tracks are well moulded with good detail and really don't need replacing. Tracks, tyres and mudflaps were touched in later by hand with thinned washes of Humbrol black after the top colour was sealed with floor polish. This method is preferred to masking as there's no risk of pulling paint off when removing tape.

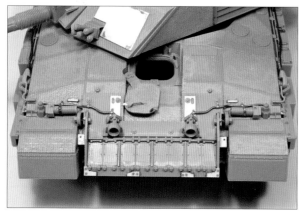

The kit provides a length of string for the tow cable, but this was replaced with copper braid left over from another project and various fittings were added with thin card and lots of Squadron Green Putty welds. Only the lower hull tub is common to both Challenger 1 and 2 kits, the upper hull and turret are all new and a clear parts' sprue for the head and tail lights is included. There's less risk of damaging the clear parts if super glue or liquid cement is not used; PVA or white glue is a safer option Tamiya haven't filled in under the side sponsons and some 1mm plastic card took care of the opening above the rear sprockets. I didn't go the full hull length as the rest can't be seen with the skirts on. A clear piece of celluloid for the vision blocks and CIP panels is in the kit with dimensions on sizes to be cut called out in the instructions. I painted the back of the vision blocks with Tamiya X27 Clear Red and Clear Green for the sights before attaching with PVA.

The road wheels from the Challenger 1 have been reworked, and new drive sprockets and one-piece armoured side skirts with canvas lower covers are well moulded. The edges of these have been thinned a little and the overlapping joins have been scored in the canvas to create the appearance of separate pieces. There aren't any mesh engine screens included although Tamiya do market these separately. Here ET Models' products have been used. The kit decals are quite adequate for the task but Echelon's T35010 Challenger 2 Operation Telic were used because of the variety they offer. These are super thin and require great care when applying.

Tamiya masking tape covered all clear parts before painting with the headlight lenses left off until the after the flat clear sealing coat was applied. All spraying was done with Tamiya colours. The model was primed with grey and then pre-shaded with black. The CIP panels were sprayed gloss white and masked off after they had dried thoroughly. Various Tamiya acrylics were then mixed for the Desert Yellow, XF-52 Flat Earth used for the dust skirts. With a sealing gloss coat applied it's time for the decals, these are super thin and required great care when applying. When these had dried overnight another gloss coat was applied to seal them and prevent any damage from the oil washes coming next. Green acrylic paint scratches were applied with the tip of a needle over high-wear areas, green and then black were dry brushed over the engine deck's rubber gun tube protectors. A thin turps wash of brown/grey oil paint was then applied over the entire model being careful to avoid the masked clear parts. This was allowed to dry and then a damp flat brush was drawn down over all vertical areas to create stains and streaks. The same wash was reapplied to all recesses and around raised details, bolts etc, allowed to dry and streaked again. The oil spot method of applying very small random dots of burnt umber and various other colours including white went on all vertical surfaces doing one panel at a time and again drawing a damp flat brush down, blending these colours in with the original dried wash. Heavily thinned XF57 Buff was air brushed over the lower half and around the rear to give it a dusty look followed with washes of Humbrol tan/brown enamels to build layers of dust and dirt. Humbrol 71 was dry brushed over the canvas dust skirts to highlight creases in the material. More scratches with dark green were added focusing. Photos show the desert yellow applied over the original green quickly wore off with use and sand storms. Deeper scratches were created with a 2B pencil around high-use areas and rubbed over the tracks' end connectors. Mud was then splattered by flicking a flat brush against a hard edge using different thinned Humbrol brown and grey enamels to add more depth to the weathering. Humbrol Matt Clear enamel was air

brushed after a final check and head light bowls were painted silver and the lens fitted with PVA to hold them in place. I had originally taped over the tail lights with the intention of removing it later, some Challenger 2 photos from that period show these lens with tape left in place so I did the same. Vision block tapes were removed and a final rub with that 2B pencil again on the track end connectors was given

CHALLENGER 2
Royal Tank Regiment, AJAX Squadron, United Kingdom 2017-present
1/35 Scale
Kirk Ashley-Morgan

This is the Trumpeter Challenger 2 Enhanced Armour kit No. 01522. However, after seeing images of the urban specialists of AJAX Squadron, of which only three ever received this colour scheme, it was decided to dispense with the heavy armour and use some aftermarket products to represent this British training tank. The Trumpeter kit was chosen because it includes the latest road wheels with lightening holes and features the non-slip texture on the hull and turret. The kit assembles reasonably well and was detailed with some scratch-building and Accurate Armour products.

The Accurate Armour Challenger 2 detail set was used to enhance the tank's features (A053). Accurate Armour carbon fibre aerials were used (A094) and the decals are a combination from the kit, from Tamiya's Challenger 2 and from Bison decals, although the latter are now made by Star Decals No. 35-C1065.

Detail on the turret top to recesses was scratch-built for the storage bins. Other scratch-built items include the handles for the fire extinguishing system, for which thin plastic rod was used.

Here the detail of the resin fuel drums can be seen.

Accurate Armour No. A114 flashing beacon lenses amber were sought and added. This orange light is mandatory on military training vehicles.

From the side the photo-etch side skirts, part of the Accurate Armour detail set, can be seen. Trumpeter has included full-armoured side skirts but these are only fitted when deployed. During training these light side skirts are standard.

The dozer blade wasn't all that easy to fit and scratch-built detail has been added to make it look more realistic in terms of the available research material.

The kit tracks were used although they are not strictly accurate for a modern Challenger 2. The fault is at the joining of the track pads and links. Aftermarket products are available to replace the tracks but at quite a cost. Since the dozer blade and side skirts would cover most of the tracks it's not always worth the investment.

Tamiya paints were used: XF1 Flat Black, XF2 Flat White, XF54 Dark Sea Grey, XF67 NATO Green, XF68 NATO Brown and XF85 Rubber Black. The detail painting was completed using various Vallejo acrylic paints; A very thin wash of AK Interactive neutral grey was used and some other areas received some light paint chipping and weathering effects. Vallejo matt varnish was used to finish the model.

The trickiest part of the build was integrating some of the resin detail. In some cases it needed untold improvement to the kit to make it work which just wasn't worthwhile and in other cases the improvement to the build was too negligible to warrant the effort.

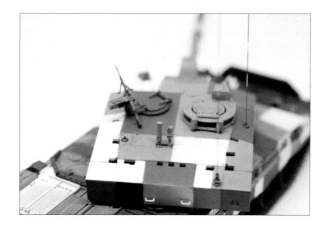

Modelling the Challenger 2

The British Army's Challenger 2 has been at the forefront for a vast majority of its all-arms activity since its adoption in 1998. Over the past 21 years Challenger 2 has seen service upholding UN mandates in the Balkans to forging the spearpoint of British ground operations in Iraq.

Challenger 2 has seen several in-service upgrades as a result of its operational experiences, culminating in the impressive theatre entry standard (TES) fit, otherwise known as 'Megatron'. For the modeller there are few upgrade options available, but those that do exist give a mouth-watering insight into the 62-tonne beast.

The modeller has several choices of kits and scales at their disposal, all with their merits and potential for super detailing and incorporating into small vignettes or large-scale dioramas. From Airfix's charming Quick Build models to Accurate Armour's beautifully rendered Challenger Armoured Repair and Recovery Vehicle (CrARRV) resin conversion kit for Tamiya's Challenger 2, the possibilities of producing a range of accurate Challenger 2s are boundless.

Model Kits of Challenger 2

Airfix Quick Build J6010, Desert Challenger 2
Airfix Quick Build J6022, Temperate (Green) Challenger 2
Bronco Challenger 2 MBT 1/35 Workable Track Link Set AB3523 (Plastic)
Dragon No. 14028, 1/144, Challenger 2 and Warrior Combi-Pack
Dragon No. 7222, 1/72 Royal Scots Dragoon Guards KFOR
Dragon No. 7285, 1/72 With Dozer Blade and ERA Side Armour
Dragon No. 7287, 1/72 With full ERA and Bar Armour
Tamiya No. 35274, 1/35 Desertized Fit
Trumpeter No. 07214, 1/72 Royal Scots Dragoon Guards KFOR
Trumpeter No. 07215, 1/72 Desertized Fit
Trumpeter No. 7222, 1/72 With Dozer Blade and ERA Side Armour KFOR
Trumpeter No. 00308, 1/35 Royal Scots Dragoon Guards KFOR
Trumpeter No. 00323, 1/35 Desertized Fit, Iraq 2003
Trumpeter No. 00345, 1/35 With Dozer Blade and ERA Side Armour KFOR
Trumpeter No. 01522, 1/35 With full ERA and Bar Armour

AIRFIX
J6010 and J6022 Quick Build Challenger 2 models

Airfix offer the Challenger 2 as a light-hearted Quick Build project that would appeal to the Challenger 2 enthusiast, the established modeller and the novice. The kits contain 35 plastic modular bricks, some with moulded details such as nose EAR armour and hatches, as well as stickers and painted sections. The kits come with rotating road wheels and single-piece tracks. Offered in two colour schemes, J6010 is finished in desert yellow while J6022 is finished in a bronze green.

Top right and above right: The Airfix J6010 assembled and exploded view. Images courtesy of Hornby

Top and above: The Airfix J6022 assembled and a view of the component parts. Images courtesy of Hornby

BRONCO
Challenger 2 MBT 1/35 Workable Track Link Set AB3523

Bronco's Challenger 2 MBT Workable Track Link Set depicts the earlier Challenger 2 track set, recognizable by its shoes' slightly sloping steel sides that face one another horizontally. The track is presented in an end-opening box with computer-generated tracks on one side and clear instructions on the back.

The kit features seven sprues moulded in brown plastic with a very straightforward construction technique of an upper and lower track section laid over the track pins. The track guides are integral to the main pad construction which simplifies overall assembly and removes the possibility of parts disappearing during construction.

The track detailing is far superior to that offered by a vinyl track set and Bronco's designers have clearly been paying attention. Nut heads have been well rendered and the steel road wheel bearing surfaces of the track have been beautifully captured.

DRAGON
Challenger 2, No. 7222, 1/72

Dragon's modelling option of the Challenger 2 is restricted to 1/72 scale, but their offering is every bit as sharp as any number of their larger 1/35 scale kits. Presented in an open-lid box, these are decorated with an interesting mix of photographs and paintings.

The photograph of kit 7222, for example, features five KFOR-marked Challenger 2s of the Royal Scots Dragoon Guards (SCOTS DG), possibly at the rear of their Pec laager near the Serbian border in Kosovo. Side illustrations feature clear side-profile photos of the completed models which is extremely useful as a reference for the modeller.

The first kit is the straightforward Challenger 2 in its 'everyday' or training configuration. The kit is supplied in sturdy grey plastic with crisp decals for SCOTS DG Challenger 2s that supported UNMIK in Kosovo as part of their 2000 Operation Agricola tour.

The kit itself isn't awash with parts, as a lot of the detail is moulded; this makes it a great subject for the new or experienced modeller. It is injection moulded in grey plastic and presented as two sprues and three separate castings for the hull and upper body. Hull details are as clear as the Trumpeter range of Challenger 2s, though Dragon have made some elements such as the stowage bins for the driver's tools separate items.

The lower hull is slightly sharper in terms of detailing and includes elements missed in Trumpeter's range. While not vital to the finish of the model, they remain a nice touch and show the great attention to detail Dragon's mould makers have exercised in their craft.

Some upper hull details have been simplified for the sake of accurate representation, especially around the rear deck. This has not only lowered the silhouette of these items but allowed for finer detailing without introducing easy-to-break weak points. A nice touch is the separate driver's hatch, which would easily allow the adventurous to add a driver figure, sadly not included, to help set the scene for a themed diorama. The side bazooka plates form part of the moulding like Trumpeter's offering and the sprocket covers are separate parts, which allow for more modelling options.

The upper turret layout is well considered with Dragon stealing a march on Trumpeter with their finer detailing. Of note is the less cumbersome-looking loader's periscope and main gun mount. The L30A1 main gun barrel is again a single-piece moulding and the twin GMPGs are beautifully rendered.

The sprues are well designed with most of the part count being taken by the road wheels and sprockets which are presented on their own sprue. The detailing is sharp and not as bold as the Trumpeter castings, with the sprockets in particular well represented. The second sprue features the lower hull mounting plate and the other elements of the kit.

Injection marks are well hidden, with only the smoke discharger mounts showing marks and the dischargers themselves have slight dimpling, easily hidden with a small amount of filler. The front glacis and rear engine plate are well moulded and present no fit issues.

The vinyl tracks and tow cabling are sharper in definition to Trumpeter's offerings and accurately portray the early style type of track.

Often accused of producing confusing instructions, Dragon presents the modeller with instructions that are a testament to great graphic design, with colour photos used throughout and pieces glow-highlighted for ease of identification. Dragon have referenced Hobby Colours, but the modeller can do no wrong with using a dark green and dark grey or NATO-coloured black paints.

The decal sheets are always well presented and well researched. Decals are beautifully rendered and well within colour register, with Dragon choosing to portray a mount of the SCOTS DG in KFOR guise. The Union Flag is correct and the inclusion of 7 Armoured Brigade's Red Jerboa is a nice, but very important touch along with the Saltire flags. Dragon has also included two decals, in gold and black, featuring the Scottish Lion rampant, as well as sharp call-sign decals.

No detail has been overlooked and with Dragon presenting a model that is slightly more finished than Trumpeter's offerings, it should be considered a must for any modeller's British armour collection.

The second kit (7285) again features a Challenger 2 of the SCOTS DG in KFOR guise; this time the kit is supplied with a wonderfully detailed dozer blade (BEMA: bulldozer earth moving attachment) and side armour, without anti-dust skirts. Dragon has also made the tracks from their DM compound and a sheet of photo-etched engine grills.

The final kit of the trio (7287) features the Challenger 2 with its ubiquitous up-armour package featuring ROMOR-A package, including nose explosive reactive armour (ERA). The extra armour is supplied as two separate pale grey sprues. Dragon has again made the tracks from their DM compound and as well as a sheet of photo-etched engine grills, they have also included a sheet of photo-etch bar armour. Of note is the smaller 1/144 scale model of the Challenger 2 (No. 14037 and 14028) which is offered as a set with an FV510 Warrior and AS90. Both of the sets are pretty generic representations and straightforward in completion. The Warrior set is supplied with KFOR markings, whilst the AS90 set features a desertized Challenger 2 with full ROMOR armour.

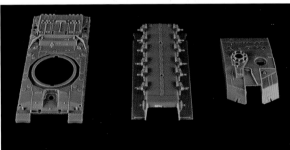

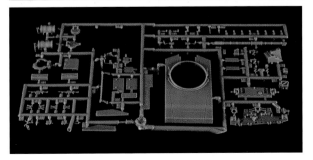

The Challenger 2 7222 kit is injection moulded in grey plastic and presented as two sprues and three separate castings for the hull and upper body.

Box art for the 7285 and 7287 kits, the Challenger 2 of the SCOTS DG with dozer blade and the Challenger 2 with its ubiquitous up-armour package respectively.

TAMIYA
1/35 Challenger 2

Presented in Tamiya's smart and beautifully illustrated packaging, the Challenger 2 kit is simply the most eye-catching of the 1/35 offerings. While offering a fair representation of the Challenger 2, the lower hull is from the previous Challenger 1 kit; the differences when compared to Trumpeter's offering is clear. This oversight may be in part due to the relatively early initial release date of 2004, although this is a year after Trumpeter's release of their range of kits.

Aside from this oversight, the kit is exceptionally well designed. It is moulded in sand-coloured plastic on five sprues with separate lower and upper hull mouldings. The tracks are moulded in vinyl plastic and give a fair representation of the early track sets. Also included in the track moulding is a small piece that sits between turret top and gun mantle replicating the rubber debris guard.

Tamiya have also included an ancillaries' pack containing a large sheet of white plastic for flat CIP panels, clear plastic for periscopes, thread for the recovery cables and polycaps for wheel sets. Also included is a length of wire for a D10 comms wire carrier on the rear of the hull.

Aided by the ever-present tank crewman, the instructions are clear and the decal selection, while not exhaustive, allows the modeller to produce one of three SCOTS DG Challengers on operations in Iraq in 2003. The sprues are well designed. Tamiya have produced a kit that will stand up well to scrutiny. The unique Challenger 2 road wheels and sprockets are particularly well rendered as are the numerous details. The thermal sleeve of the two-part L30 main gun and the details of the loader's GPMG are beautifully defined as are the anti-dust skirts of the ROMOR skirt armour.

The upper hull is beautifully cast, with details such as the refuelling caps being sharper than the Challenger 1. The front glacis plate features some fine welding lines, whilst the rear decks are nicely finished. For added detail Tamiya also produce a Challenger 2 photo-etched set of mesh covers for the rear deck louvers.

The turret is a truly amazing piece of observational art. A very straightforward construction process delivers a square and realistic turret, with fine details such as manufacturing marks and delicately raised bolt heads. A particularly nice detail is the gun mantle with the overhead TOG sight. These have been well engineered and the TOG sight is designed to allow the modeller to show the sight's armoured door both open and closed.

Two figures are included that represent the commander and loader attired in period combats and body armour, without feet, meaning their use as external props is somewhat curtailed. My only quibbles are lack of detailing on the rear of the road wheels and the all-important anti-slip covering for both upper hull and turret. Though easily rectified, these details would have made Tamiya's wonderful kit a truly remarkable one.

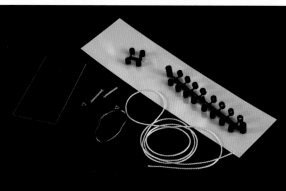

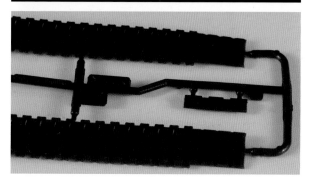

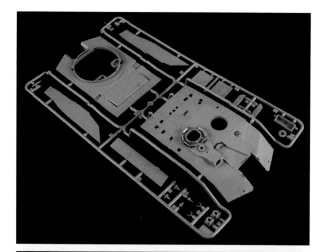

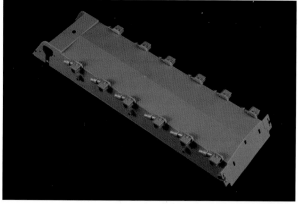

The lower hull is from the previous Challenger 1 kit; the differences when compared to Trumpeter's offering (TrVsTa001) is clear. Aside from this oversight the kit is well designed. The upper hull (Tam 35274 003) is beautifully cast, with details such as the refuelling caps being sharper than the Challenger 1. Unfortunately the non-slip texture on the hull and turret is missing from this kit.

TRUMPETER
Challenger 2 Range

1/72 scale

Trumpeter has really pulled out the stops for their fantastic range of 1/72-scale Challenger 2s offering the modeller three very different versions. The kits are all presented in sturdy lid-opening boxes which feature photographs of the complete plastic models in a clean state on the lid top and well-drawn examples of the contained model on the side panels.

The first kit (07214) is the straightforward Challenger 2 in its 'everyday' or training configuration. The kit is supplied in sturdy grey plastic with crisp decals for the Royal Scots Dragoon Guards (SCOTS DG) Challenger 2s that supported UNMIK in Kosovo as part of their 2000 Operation Agricola tour.

The second kit (07215) features the Challenger 2 of the Royal Tank Regiment (RTR) in early Operation Telic configuration with its ubiquitous up-armour package featuring ROMOR-A package, including nose explosive reactive armour (ERA). The side armour is supplemented with its unique anti-dust skirts and well generic in-theatre decals. The extra armour is supplied as two separate pale grey sprues.

The final kit of the trio (07216) again features a Challenger 2 of the SCOTS DG in KFOR guise; the kit is supplied with a wonderfully detailed dozer blade (BEMA) and side armour, without anti-dust skirts.

The baseline kit consists of two light grey plastic-injection-moulded sprues. The details are crisp and the layout is well thought-out. The L30A1 main gun barrel is a single-piece moulding whilst the road wheels are delightfully executed and accessories are moulded directly onto key parts, such as the spare tracks on the rear engine plate.

The turret and hull are of two-part construction and fit together with the use of some pretty heavy-duty locating lugs. The L30A1 gun mount is able to be elevated and sits squarely in the turret. The turret and hull mouldings are rendered exceptionally well, with some amazing attention to detail from the mould makers, in particular the lower hull with its centreline reinforcement strip and detailed road wheel mounts.

The upper hull is essentially a well-executed miniature version of the 1/35 and is well rendered, though the upper engine cover arm is a little thick; this by no means detracts from the appearance. The turret top is clean and sits squarely on the lower part and is complete with the mid-production pintle mount GPMG.

For the vinyl elements of the kit Trumpeter have chosen to mould not only the tracks, but also the recovery cables in the black vinyl. The detail is as sharp as can be expected of the scale and gives more than a fair representation of the early-type track work.

Moving onto the instructions, in all three cases these are clear and concise and follow a logical order. Trumpeter use Gunze Sangyo Mr Color as a reference, but given the familiarity of British Army paint schemes, the modeller can do no wrong with simply using a dark green and dark grey or NATO-coloured black paints.

The decal sheets are well presented and researched. The Union Flag is correct and 7 Armoured Brigade's Red Jerboa is included, an important touch along with the Royal Scots Dragoon Guards Saltire flags.

Again, no detail has been overlooked and Trumpeter have delivered a great selection of Challenger 2s that punch above their weight in terms of quality and finish and are by no means intimidating to the modeller.

1/35 scale

Trumpeter's 1/35 range of scale Challenger 2 models echoes their 1/72 offerings with the exception of kit No. 01522 which features bar armour as well as the ROMOR fit. Trumpeter also offer the modeller their own label-workable track for early examples of Challenger 2 with kit No. 02043. Such is the appeal of Trumpeter's Challenger 2 model that it has been re-boxed in the past by both Airfix and Hobbycraft.

All kits are presented with a painted diorama, sadly unsigned, which owes as much to artistic licence as they do imagination. It is the side illustrations though that really steal the show with their sharp and reasonably accurate depictions of the Challenger 2.

The baseline kit (00308) is the straightforward Challenger 2 it is 'everyday' or training configuration. The kit is supplied as six sturdy green plastic sprues, separate hull and turret top and bottoms, vinyl track and polycaps for the wheel sets. Decals are crisp, representing Challenger 2s of the SCOTS DG that supported UNMIK in Kosovo as part of their 2000 Operation Agricola tour.

The second kit (00323) features the Challenger 2, again of SCOTS DG in Operation Telic configuration with its ubiquitous up-armour package featuring ROMOR package. The kit is supplied as six sturdy desert-yellow plastic sprues, with separate hull and turret top and bottoms, vinyl track, thread for recovery cabling and polycaps for the wheel sets. The side armour is supplemented with its unique anti-dust skirts as well as simple generic in-theatre decals.

The third kit (07216) again features a Challenger 2 of the SDG in KFOR guise; this time the kit is supplied with a wonderfully detailed dozer blade (BEMA: bulldozer earth moving attachment) and side armour, without anti-dust skirts. The kit is supplied as seven sturdy green plastic sprues, separate hull and turret top and bottoms, vinyl track and polycaps for the wheel sets. Simple generic in-theatre decals are also provided.

The final kit (01522) is supplied as eight sturdy pale grey plastic sprues, with separate hull and turret top and bottoms, vinyl track, thread for recovery cabling and polycaps for the wheel sets. It also features a small photo-etch sheet and a cardboard sheet printed with standard ration pack graphics. As a kit option, the nose ERA armour can be replaced with a dozer blade.

The kits themselves are well presented with clear pictorial instructions, which is a big help as some of the instruction translations are a little wide of the mark. The construction is broken down into 22 stages and each is relatively straightforward, which means the model can be made by novice and veteran alike.

The track is well moulded and depicts an early track set. What's interesting is that Trumpeter have added four separate position lugs for the two attachment apertures. This may be in response to claims that the tracks of earlier kits were too long.

Moving onto the plastic elements of the kits, they're sharp with only the odd poorly located sink mark in mouldings. The road wheels are worthy of note as Trumpeter have chosen to mould detailing on the hull side disks, a detail Tamiya have overlooked.

The lower section is well designed with the reinforcement strip running down the length of the hull. Another welcome touch is the inclusion of blanking plates that pretty much hide the void of the upper hull when it's added.

The upper hull is well moulded, with noticeable anti-slip surface finish on those parts of the hull where it is traditionally applied. The detail moulding of refuelling caps and disks is a little flat, but easily remedied with careful application of a blade around their circumference. The engine bay grills and louvres are well moulded and the engine cover is a separate item, complete with anti-slip covering.

The turret is a little more complex in construction than Tamiya's offering, featuring separate tool bins, which would allow for some interesting modelling options. Moulding is otherwise sharp, but the loader's periscope appears to be a little too small, so is an opportunity for a scratch-built remedy. Of note are the slightly untidy weld lines near the gun mantle, well observed and showing the human input into the construction of the Challenger 2. Be aware of the unfortunately placed sink marks in both the

commander's and loader's hatches. Sadly, the excellent anti-slip finish featured on the hull doesn't extend to the turret, which, whilst easily sorted, is a bit of a disappointment.

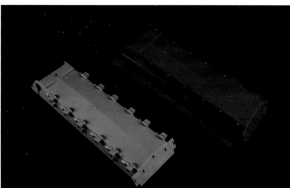

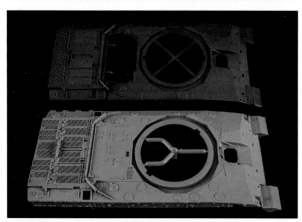

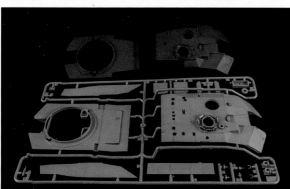

These images compare the Trumpeter (back) and Tamiya (front) kits.

The remaining parts are well moulded with the L30 main gun and sights being supplied as a six-part construction; the twin GPMGs are accurate and interestingly Trumpeter have opted to mould the recovery cables as opposed to supplying thread.

The recommended finish is standard two-tone British armour, though it would look equally good in BATUS sand and green finish. The decal sheet, which is quite a size, allows the modeller to choose several finishing options, including a KFOR vehicle and a range of your own call signs using some thoughtfully supplied digits and letters in yellow.

Overall a great kit ready for super detailing as well as perfecting your general model-making skills on.

Aftermarket Kit Manufacturers

As with all things modelling, there are numerous concerns that offer additional detailing kits including decals. To make life easier I've split these details into separate modelling areas and given a brief overview of each manufacturer's output. Items are still available at time of print, but may change due to market requirements.

Generic Fittings and Fixtures

Accurate Armour numerous 1/35 multi-media kits and upgrades including CrARRV conversion kit for 1/35 Tamiya (Resin and Metal)
Bronco Challenger 2 MBT 1/35 Workable Track Link Set AB3523 (Plastic)
Eduard 35565 Challenger 2 for 1/35 Trumpeter Kits (Photo-Etch)
ET Models EA35-110 Challenger 2 Grills for 1/35 Tamiya (Photo-Etch)
Fruilmodels ATL-163 Challenger 2 Early Type Track 1/35 (White Metal)
Fruilmodels ATL-179 Challenger 2 Later Type Track 1/35 (White Metal)
Lion Mark LAM031 Challenger 2 Metal Mesh Set for 1/35 Tamiya (Photo-Etch)
Lion Mark LM20000 Challenger 2 Barrel for 1/35 Tamiya (Resin and Metal)
Panzer Art RE35-070 Challenger 2 Spare Wheels Challenger 2 for 1/35 Tamiya (Resin)
Panzer Art RE35-079 Road Wheels Challenger 2 for 1/35 Tamiya (Resin)
R-Model 35130 Challenger 2 Early Type Track 1/35 (White Metal)
Tamiya 35277 Challenger 2 Grills 1/35 (Photo-Etch)
Trumpeter Challenger 2 MBT 1/35 Workable Track Link Set TR60 (Plastic)
Voyager Model FE35013 Challenger 2 Grills for 1/35 Tamiya (Photo-Etch)
Voyager PEA222 Challenger 2 (Later) Grills for 1/35 Tamiya (Photo-Etch)

Theatre-Specific Upgrades
Kosovo Era
Accurate Armour numerous 1/35 multi-media kits and upgrades
Extra Tech EXV72079 1/72 Dragon (Photo-Etch)

Iraq Era
Accurate Armour numerous 1/35 multi-media kits and upgrades
Echelon T35010 British Challenger 2s in Operation Telic (2 RTR) (Decals)
Eduard 35743 Challenger 2 for 1/35 Tamiya (Photo-Etch)

Eduard 36126 Challenger 2 Enhanced armour for 1/35 Trumpeter (Photo-Etch)

ET Models E35-237 Challenger 2 desertized for 1/35 Tamiya (Photo-Etch)

Star Decals 35-C-1096 Royal Scots Dragoon Guards Iraq 2003

Star Decals 35-C-1099 Queens Royal Hussars Iraq 2003 and 2004

Voyager PE35374 Challenger 2 desertized for 1/35 Tamiya (Photo-Etch)

Voyager PE35388 Modern British Challenger 2 for 1/35 Trumpeter 001522 (Photo-Etch)

Voyager PEA188 Challenger 2 Combat Identification Panel (CIP) GP (Photo-Etch)

Resin and Multi-Media Kits

Accurate Armour

The range of multi-media Challenger 2 upgrade kits offered by Accurate Armour is simply the best on offer to the modeller. Indeed, such is the quality of their work they are suppliers of models to the UK defence industry. Whether you're new to upgrading your 1/35 kit or a seasoned modeller detailing a Queen's Royal Hussars Challenger in Basra, there are plentiful options to spark the imagination. Of particular interest is set A085 featuring a complete set of damaged Challenger 2 road wheels that will fit either the Tamiya or Trumpeter models.

The quality of the resin remains consistently high with no casting bubbles or blow-out; the details in objects cast in resin are truly astounding. The photo-etch does seem to be slightly thicker when compared to other manufacturers, and the detailing is, in some cases, sharper.

A great example of how all of Accurate Armour's items come together is in their update kit for Trumpeter's SCG KFOR Challenger 2 (00308) kit. A053 helps the modeller produce Challenger 2 in its tank park configuration. The kits contain an array of finely produced resin items (A053001-004), photo-etch side skirts and detailing elements, brass recovery cable and a length of brass rod (A053005 and 006). The instructions (A053007-010) are clear, utilizing photographs of parts in situ as opposed to possibly confusing graphics. After careful examination, most modellers will be able to produce a more accurate 'everyday' version of the Challenger 2.

If you're looking for something entirely different then look no further than the Challenger Armoured Repair and Recovery Vehicle (CrARRV) kit (C024). This is based on the Challenger 1 MBT, and first saw action in the Gulf War of 1991. The CrARRV carries all the necessary equipment to maintain, recover and repair the Challenger 2 MBT, as well as having the ability to dig all-important hull-down fire positions.

This kit produces a vehicle that will convert Tamiya's Challenger 2 (No. 35274) into the latest vehicles using the double-pin track and sprockets; for added accuracy Accurate Armour's road wheel sets (A084 or A085) can be added.

The conversion includes a new hull top, crane, dozer blade, etched brass skirt-plate system, and all tools necessary to produce a CrARRV. When mated with the excellent Challenger 2 Power Pack model (A148), the modelling possibilities are truly endless.

As well as resin and photo-etch parts Accurate Armour also does a series of beautifully rendered decals printed by Fantasy Printshop. Set DEK053G features markings for 2 RTR, SDG as well as the Queen's Royal Lancers. Set DEK053 is a more generic set of decals,

which would suit a range of vehicles including the CrARRV conversion kit in UN guise. There is a final set, primarily for the CrARRV (Dec024) which features stencilling for SFOR, KFOR and IFOR.

Lion Mark

Lion Mark's LM20000 upgrade kit for Tamiya's L30 main gun is a six-part offering of aluminium and resin. Well observed and beautifully designed, this simple kit really does bring the L30 gun alive. Of note is the subtle dimpling of the thermal sleeves and delicate sag of the rubber lower barrel shroud. The fume extractor is nicely replicated whilst the muzzle reference system mirror and shroud are well cast and sit squarely on top of the muzzle.

Panzer Art

Polish manufacturer Panzer Art produces some of the clearest cast-resin wheels on the market and with their Challenger 2 offerings they don't disappoint. Producing two unique sets, RE35-070 spare wheels and RE35-079 depicting the earlier Challenger 2 road wheels, Panzer Art's attention to detail is to be applauded. The subtle texture on the surfaces of both sets is well cast; also of note is the beautiful rear wheel detailing on set RE35-079.

Decals

Echelon T35010 British Challenger 2s in Operation Telic (2 RTR)

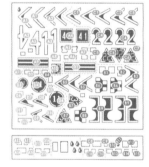

Echelon has a well-established reputation among British armour enthusiasts, with good reason. Their KFOR Challenger 1 decal set was well researched and beautifully produced. Their subsequent Challenger 2 decal set has raised the bar considerably, offering the modeller the chance to model five separate Challengers with 12 overall options and a host of generic markings found on the Challenger 2.

All the decal sets are for those Challengers engaged in Operation Telic roles (UK parlance for Operation Iraqi Freedom) with a great emphasis on Royal Tank Regiment (RTR) vehicles. Of note is the length that Echelon has gone to, to reproduce vehicle registration numbers of Challenger 2s that exist, a detail many manufacturers often overlook.

Printed by Microscale, USA, all options accurately capture the subtle differences exhibited by each of the sample vehicles. The decal colours are as sharp as always with the blacks being represented at around 80 percent grey, the Union Flags are correctly printed and the friendly forces recognition chevron is offered in varying styles.

Echelon have also included the emblems of Badger, Cyclops and Egypt squadrons and the all-important Jerboa of 7 Armoured Brigade that allows for some personalization and diorama possibilities away from the Gulf and Afghan theatres of operations.

Star Decals 35-C-1096 and 35-C-1099

Star Decals of Sweden have produced two completely differing sets of decals representing Challenger 2 during two very distinct phases of Operation Telic. Set 35-C-1096 represents four Challenger 2s of the Royal Scots Dragoon Guards (SCOTS DG) during the Invasion of Iraq in 2003.

Set 35-C-1099 represents five Challenger 2s of the Queen's Royal Hussars (QRH) during their 2003 and 2004 tours of Iraq. The QRH set is of particular interest as it offers the modeller some interesting modelling options as well as some distinctive markings. These including a unique marking reminiscent of the seal of the Deutsches Afrikakorps displayed on a vehicle based at Amarah in August 2004.

Again, both sets are well researched, with Star producing a clear and concise decal location chart for all modelling options and the decals themselves are well laid out for the modeller. Star have opted to print the black details at an 80 percent grey finish which gives the modeller a great set of scale-coloured finishes that would be otherwise hard to achieve.

Etch and White Metal Kits

The one thing Challenger 2 is not short of is etch, which focuses predominantly on the engine grills. There are sets by a range of manufacturers for both the Tamiya and Trumpeter 1/35 models and a single set, by Extratech, for Dragon's 1/72 series of models.

Eduard

Eduard, whose name is as well known in the detailing world of modelling as Tamiya is in the production of model kits, have produced three unique sets of photo-etch for the Challenger 2.

The first set is No. 35565, a generic upgrade set for the Trumpeter version of the Challenger 2. Featuring three frets of beautifully cut metal, this set really brings out the best in Trumpeter's offering, addressing well some of the detailing shortcomings, in particular the turret and rear upper hull.

Set No. 36126 is also for the Trumpeter Challenger 2, in particular the Operation Telic kit No. 01522. Supplied on two frets, the kit's main focus is to replace the bulky plastic bar armour with more scale-realistic photo-etch. It also features the longer anti-dust guards for the rear of the hull.

The final set is No. 35743 designed for the Tamiya Challenger 2. Supplied as two frets, this set's main features are upgrades for the CIP panels and rear deck areas. Also supplied are details such as the actuator arm of the TOG sight's armoured door and handles for the skirting armour packs.

ET Models

ET Models are a prolific Shanghai-based photo-etch manufacturer whose upgrade kit (E35-237) for the Tamiya Challenger 2 pulls no punches. Spread across six frets, this set really does take Tamiya's Challenger 2 to the next level in terms of super detailing. From the spare fuel drum ratchets to the commander's cupola, no part of the kit is left untouched.

The designers tackle all the usual elements for upgrade, such as fuel filler caps, with finesse, but where ET Models really stand out is in the anti-dust skirts for the ROMOR armour. As per the prototype the skirts are made from separate sheets of metal, which enable the modeller to produce more accurate in-theatre models where these skirts would sometimes come adrift. The three-page instructions are beautifully drawn and clear, following a logical order.

If the E35-237 kit is a little too complex then the single-fret engine grill cover set (EA35-110) is as equally sharp as its larger counterpart. It allows the modeller to add a nice detailing touch to the rear deck without altering the form of the model greatly.

Extratech

Extratech predominantly produce photo-etch for aircraft modellers, so set EXV72079 would suit Dragon's 1/72 kit No. 7287 as an aid to converting it to an Operation Telic fit. The single fret includes remodelled rear dust flaps, front of turret CIP panels and engine deck mesh.

Voyager Model

Voyager Model are producers of multi-media detailing kits for the armour modeller, offering no less than five upgrade kits for the Challenger 2. Kits PEA222 and FE35013 are both engine deck grill upgrades for Tamiya's Challenger 2, whilst kit PEA188 is a generic CIP panel upgrade kit. All three are supplied as single sprue, are well engineered and show great attention to detail.

Kit PE35374 is a well-designed multi-media kit for Tamiya's Challenger 2. It features no less than nine frets of photo-etch, resin tow-cable eyes and fire extinguishers as well as a selection of rods and cables. Well designed, the set adds life to Tamiya's offering whilst using as many of the original kit's parts as possible. This not only reduces unnecessary waste, but also speeds up build time. One detail that sticks out is the wonderful texturing on the fuel drum securing straps.

Fret set PE35388 is a full kit set designed for Trumpeter's 1/35 Challenger 2 No. 01522. Again, a multi-fret, multi-media design which brings the Trumpeter Operation Telic model up to spec with both photo-etch up-detailing and upgrading the bar armour on the rear of the vehicle. A well-researched kit, it presents the modeller with a real challenge, especially with the rear hull hanging bar armour. Set PEA200 is also available and simply replaces the Trumpeter bar armour.

Friulmodel

Friulmodel white metal armoured vehicle track has a hard-won reputation as being the best in the market and it's with good reason. The tracks are always well researched and reflect types of track used by vehicles over certain periods, with Challenger 2 being no different. Set ATL-163 features 160 track links and wire to produce the earlier pattern track, whilst set ATL-179 again features 160 track links and wire that produce the later type of track.

R-Model

R-Model are another Chinese model kit upgrade manufacturer specializing in white metal tracks for AFVs. Their early Challenger 2 set is an interesting kit. Whilst not as sharp in detail as Friulmodel kits, the impression is definitely there, and makes for a good alternative to Friulmodel.

As with all things this list is purely contemporaneous and is subject to change. Two key suppliers of resin-based detailing kits, but not included due to closure, are Cromwell Models and Castoff Models. Cromwell produced a range of 1/72 Challenger 2s, including the TES Megatron version, while Castoff produced the 1/35 version, as well as ROMOR up-armour kit for Trumpeter Challenger 2s. (Still RK001). The products of both of these manufacturers are much sought after by enthusiasts and collectors alike. Sadly, these amazing editions are becoming increasingly rare, but worth seeking out nonetheless, if only their unique subject matter.

A loader from the RDG using the loader's drill trainer. In this shot he has completed all the drills to load the L30, picked up the next projectile to load – in this case a replica HESH round – and he is now closing the safety shield to the rear. On firing, this shield will automatically be returned forward and the breech will be opened automatically. (Rob Griffin courtesy of RDG)

The loader is now moving across to load the projectile into the breech, which he will follow with the charge and then close the breech to load the L30. While using this trainer, the instructor can induce faults for the loader to diagnose and rectify. (Rob Griffin courtesy of RDG)

The Omani Challenger 2 in plan. The .50 can be seen and also the single-pin tracks; note the large louvres on the hull rear plate. (Peter Breakspear)

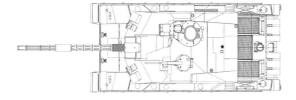

The .50 Browning mount as fitted to the Omani Challenger 2 in preference to the 7.62mm GPMG. (Peter Breakspear)

Right: Rear view of the Omani Challenger 2 variant. Note single-pin track, large rear louvres and the air-conditioning louvre on the right side; the spare track links and tools have been moved to both sides of the tank. (Peter Breakspear)

Below: Left rear view of an Omani Challenger 2. Note the jerrycan stowage and the just-visible rear louvres, plus the tools now mounted on the side. (Peter Breakspear)

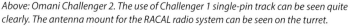

Above: Omani Challenger 2. The use of Challenger 1 single-pin track can be seen quite clearly. The antenna mount for the RACAL radio system can be seen on the turret.

Above right: The very distinctive rear of the Omani Challenger 2, showing the louvre layout and the raised rear decks. Note the long mudflaps on the rear wings and the jerrycan stowage behind the light clusters. (Peter Breakspear)

This is preferred to a fan-belt drive system. To aid cooling of the gearbox, a larger-than-normal heat exchanger has been fitted.

Another way to distinguish the Omani Challengers is to look at the right-hand side towards the rear. Located there is a grill which is part of the crew air-conditioning unit fitted to the tank. This unit takes the place of one of the fuel cells, which means that the tank carries less fuel than a British Challenger, roughly around 17 percent less. Unlike the British version, the fuel panniers were replaced by a sealed compartment system. This proved so effective that it was subsequently incorporated into the British Trojan and Titan engineer vehicles which we will look at later on. To help make up for the loss of fuel by the fitting of the air-conditioner system, two approach fuel drums, each holding roughly 180 litres, are carried on the rear of the tank. However, unlike the British version, they have to be carried on the top of the rear deck due to the large louvres fitted to the rear plate. The design allows for them to be discarded once used. They can also be discarded in combat as they can hinder gun movement over the

Left: The preferred loader weapon as used by Omani forces, the old but still totally effective .50 Browning machine gun. (Peter Breakspear)

Below: A fine head-on shot of an Omani Challenger 2 at speed, illustrating the conditions in which it operated. British Challengers failed during Exercise Saif Sareea II, as they were not designed for such conditions. At least lessons were learned. (Peter Breakspear)

Again, this shot illustrates the dusty conditions encountered in Oman and most desert countries. (Peter Breakspear)

rear decks. The knock-on effect of this is that the tools normally stowed on the rear plate are now stowed on the hull's left side.

Another quite obvious change is the loss of the loader's 7.62mm GPMG to be replaced by the perennial favourite M2 Browning .50 machine gun. This is mounted on a simple pintle on the loader's side. It shows that the design which entered United States service in 1930 was sound as it is still in use in many forms today. Originally one of the versions was the Ranging Gun used in Chieftain prior to the introduction of the laser rangefinder. The internal stowage was modified slightly to accept stowage for the larger ammunition of the Browning. In Dick Taylor's Haynes manual on Challenger 2 he recounts a nice little gem about the Challenger's introduction into service with the Omani Armoured Corps. He relates that the soldiers were cynical about the perceived complexity of the Challenger, for they were used to the relatively much simpler American M60 and their British Chieftains. Possibly one reason for their apparent conversion was during acceptance commissioning when they were amazed at the impact that the L23 APFDS had on the hard targets down range, made more intimate when you consider that the hard targets used were in fact their own Chieftains. He says that over the time the Omanis have become very efficient in their use of the Challenger and they use it aggressively, in training. Sadly, this success story which it was hoped would be repeated was the only external sale and although Challenger 2 took part in trials for the Greek Army in its Challenger 2E format, it was not be a winner.

The list of potential customers included Saudi Arabia, Australia and Sweden. Although Vickers gave a presentation to the Swedes, the tank was not offered come completion time. Qatar also expressed an interest in the tank but again never took it up. At first this might seem a big disappointment for all concerned. It was,

but it would be unfair to blame the tank. Often countries looking for a new tank will look at what is out there on the market and see if it meets their requirements, which may well differ from the producing nation. Greece was another country very interested in the Challenger and it took part in the trials but against Leclerc, Leopard 2, M1A1 Abrams, T80 and Ukrainian T84, a fair selection of different tanks. There has always been controversy about the conduct of the trials, but it seems that the Greeks had already decided on the German Leopard 2 and ran the trials to look as if they were still deciding.

One of the criticisms levelled at the tank was it was just that bit slower in loading compared to those with fixed ammunition, which will always be the case. The Challenger 2 that was entered was very different to the one used by the British or the Omanis. It had the CV12 powerpack totally replaced by the installation of an MTU M883 1,500bhp diesel connected to a Renk automatic transmission. This combination had several advantages over the CV12/TN54 arrangement in the in-service vehicle. As the unit was mounted transversely, it took up less room than the service version. It was also mounted on rails that would allow the whole pack to be removed from the rear of the tank once the rear plate was dropped, making pack change easier. The space saved could be used to increase either fuel or ammunition carried. In the driver's cab the traditional steering levers were replaced by an aircraft-type wheel and for the first time a forward-looking camera for the driver was fitted. This eventually became part of the upgrade and is now seen on many British fighting vehicles. The commander now had a fully panoramic stabilized day/night sight, as did the gunner. This is what the original design called for way back in the beginning of Challenger 2. However, all this was to no avail, as the Greeks had set their eyes on Leopard 2 and that is the tank that won. Since then Challenger 2 has not been fielded in any export drive.

Challenger 2 Specialist Variants

As is usual, specialist variants are produced from the current in-service hull. This make good sense in that it reduces training on different vehicles, can reduce support and logistic costs, and brings commonality to the systems. It is so for Challenger 2, which has three specialist variants built on its basic chassis.

The first we look at is the Driver Training Tank (DTT). This is a further derivative of

This 62 KK 96 is one of five service Challengers converted to the driver training role; the remainder of the DTT fleet are purpose-built hulls.
(Challenger Tank Appreciation Society)

the Challenger 1 version and while they look very similar, there have been changes to the Challenger 2 version. Some of these include a lighter hull which was achieved by building it from thinner plates and making it unarmoured, although at least five service gun tanks are also known to have been converted. The order for the vehicles was placed in December 1991 and by the end of the production run there were twenty-two Driver Training Tanks in service. These provide a valuable aid to successful training, with no more trainees having to sit outside in the wet for their turn to drive.

The hull of the in-service vehicle has usually been used to provide specialized Royal Engineer support vehicles and Challenger 2 has had two vehicles produced using the basic hull components. They provide the Royal Engineers with an Armoured Vehicle Launched Bridge (AVLB) known as Titan, and an Armoured Vehicle Royal Engineers (AVRE) known as Trojan. Both vehicles replaced the long-serving and very successful Chieftain variants which had served the Engineers faithfully and had actually been deployed on combat operations with them. But as much as there was a sort of love–hate relationship with them, they had really reached their end of life. They could not keep up with

Challenger 2 and the spares issue was becoming a problem.

Both types of vehicle are important in an all-arms battle. Without them obstacles cannot be cleared or crossed without great difficulty. The Titan is the AVLB variant and is based on a hull that is a different shape to suit the AVLB role but still using Challenger 2 components. It can carry all three of the current vehicle-launched bridges: No. 10, which is a scissors-type bridge, No. 11, which is a single-span bridge and No. 12, also is a single-span bridge. Currently there are two ways of launching bridges from armoured vehicles. The German version based on Leopard 2 carries the sections horizontally and when ready to launch, one section is pushed forward until the other section drops into place and is locked in place; the launching arm then moves forward and the bridge travels over it till it is laid. This has the tactical advantage of keeping the operation in a low-key mode unlike the British who employ the up-and-over version. The disadvantage with the German method is that the crossing span is not as great as the British system. Titan launches its bridges by approaching the gap to be crossed, then the first hydraulic ram lowers the front till the support base is firmly on the ground. Another ram then proceeds to raise the bridge to a vertical position. Then the final stage will push the bridge from the vertical position until it is horizontal. In the case of the No. 10 bridge – the scissors bridge in two halves hinged in the centre – it gives a much larger crossing capability than the other two single-span bridges. Once the scissors are in the vertical position, further movement during lowering causes the two halves to separate aided by struts and cables. Further lowering will allow the bridge to join as one span and finally it is laid across the gap. Once the bridges are laid, the Titan will reverse from the bridge location and take cover, while the main forces cross. Depending on the tactics being used, it can then either cross and follow on and be resupplied with a new bridge later or it can simply pick up the one it has just laid and carry on. The beauty of the system is that at no time does a crewmember have to exit the vehicle either during launching or recovery.

The No. 10 bridge can span a gap of over 24 metres. No. 11 can span 14.5 metres and No. 12 can span 12 metres. As noted, the Titan can collect spare bridges which are carried on an eight-wheeled bridge transporter as part of the engineer train. It can carry one No. 10 bridge or two No. 12 bridges. If the gap is more than the No. 10 can cross, a trestle kit can be used. This is placed into the gap to be crossed and the end of the No. 10 bridge is laid onto it. Another Titan then crosses the bridge and lays another No. 10 to complete the gap crossing. Using this method, crossings of up to 45 metres can be achieved. Titan can

The single-span bridge being launched from Titan is now passing the vertical; in the next stage rams will lower it to the floor. (Plain Military)

The single-span bridge starting to be raised on the Titan Royal Engineer Variant. Based on Challenger 2, Titan can carry and lay three bridge types: one scissors type and two single spans. (Plain Military)

also carry two No. 12 bridges on top of each other.

Titan with its bridges fitted is a rather large vehicle and consideration has to be given when planning road routes. The vehicle is lightly armed with a machine

This is Titan launching the No. 10 scissors bridge; clearly visible are wires and struts that allow the bridge to open. (Plain Military)

In this shot Titan is seen either laying a No. 10 bridge or collecting a prepositioned one. (Plain Military)

Below: The Pearson mine plough dismounted from the vehicle; both Titan and Trojan are capable of carrying this effective plough. (Simon Munnery, Challenger Tank Appreciation Society)

Titan showing the method for carrying two single-span bridges. In use it would lower both bridges, the bottom one would be detached and then the first would be laid over the obstacle; then Titan then would collect the second for the next crossing. (Simon Munnery, Challenger Tank Appreciation Society)

gun and personal crew weapons. Cameras are fitted to aid the driver in manoeuvring when closed down. Titan can reach road speeds of up to 59kph, which must be frightening should you be travelling the opposite direction. Titan can also be fitted with the Pearson full-width mine plough or other equipment to support the engineer role.

Trojan is the other Royal Engineer specialist vehicle using a specially built hull and again making use of most of Challenger 2 components. Trojan's role is that of

Trojan at the Tank Museum circuit at Bovington, clearly showing the travelling position of both the mine plough and the fascine. (Simon Munnery, Challenger Tank Appreciation Society)

A good rear view showing the bucket, fascine and the rear louvres on Trojan. (Plain Military)

This is Trojan using its excavator bucket to either lift or remove a pipe fascine from its stowage on the rear decks. The Pearson mine plough can be seen at the front in its deployed role.
(Simon Munnery, Challenger Tank Appreciation Society)

the Armoured Vehicle Royal Engineers (AVRE). Thirty-three Trojans are in service and perform a variety of engineer support roles. These include filling small gaps by means of the fascine that it can carry on the rear decks. Fascines were first used by tanks in the First World War when they were simply large piles of saplings bound together and carried on top of a tank. When a gap was encountered, the fascine was allowed to fall forward into the gap and then the tank could cross. These days the fascine is usually made of plastic pipe, more environmentally friendly and durable. Trojan can be fitted with a dozer blade or Pearson full-width mine plough. It is also equipped with a hydraulic excavator arm based on the civilian CAT 315 arm. This can be used for many tasks including as

crane to lift the fascine from the rear decks. Trojan is also capable of towing the wheeled trailer mounting the Python mine-clearing system. This in effect is a large explosive-filled hose that is fired into the minefield by a rocket. Once it has landed, it is detonated and can clear a lane up to 200 metres long and wide, enough for a tank to cross although care still needs to be taken. Trojan is lightly armed with an overhead remote weapon station with 7.62mm GPMG. It also has to the on-board smoke generators of the tank. Beside towing the Python trailer, it is also capable of towing the AVRE trailer, which is a four-wheel trailer used to carry a multitude of Engineers' stores.

The introduction of these two vehicles gave the Royal Engineers a big boost in battlefield capabilities.

Rear view of Trojan towing the empty engineers' trailer that contains the Python mine-clearing device. The carrier for the rocket is the object on the rear of the trailer; the explosive-filled hose would be carried inside the trailer.
(Plain Military)

In Service and In Action

With Challenger 2 now in service and with Operation Granby (Gulf War 1) fresh in everyone's minds, many must have considered whether the tank would ever again be used in such numbers in such a free-ranging role as they had in Iraq. The answer to that was soon to come. With the fall of the Berlin Wall on 9 November 1989, and the rapid collapse of the Soviet empire, many were saying the age of the main battle tank was over, that the threat was gone. They could not have been more wrong.

Challenger 2 was to soon find itself involved in two peacekeeping operations and a war. The former Yugoslavia erupted into civil war in March 1992, with three factions all hell bent on destroying each other. The world watched in horror as modern genocide unfolded. The ineffectual United Nations sent in a protection force, which was hampered by too-rigid UN regulations. In the end NATO were deployed with a much firmer hand and soon showed they were willing to meet force with force, something the UN had tried to avoid. Eventually things started to settle down and it looked as if peace had slowly started to return to the region.

Then a fresh crisis broke out in Kosovo, and again British armoured units found themselves deployed in a peacekeeping role. The first armoured units had deployed to Kosovo with Challenger 1, with KFOR (Kosovo Force) painted onto the side armour, in what was known as Operation Agricola. The Scots Dragoon Guards (SCOTS DG) were the first unit to deploy using Challenger 2 on operations, although only one squadron deployed with the tank, the remainder being employed in a dismounted role. KFOR hoped that by only deploying a small number of tanks – keeping a low profile while exercising the option to decisively engage – would be enough of a deterrent for the hostile factions. B Squadron was used to patrol areas between the warring factions and to act as a highly visible deterrent. Some of the SCOTS DG Kosovo patrols travelled distances in the region of 250 kilometres. Thankfully, throughout the whole operation, they were not called on to use their tank weaponry. Generally, their appearance was sufficient to quell any trouble. Challenger 2 demonstrated an impressive reliability despite the weight of extra armour. The KFOR Challenger 2s carried the upgraded Chobham modular side armour and ROMOR reactive armour arrays on the hull front. Several vehicles were also fitted with the Pearson combat dozer blade.

Following this, Challenger 2 found itself again deployed to the former Yugoslavia, as part of SFOR (Stabilization Force in Bosnia and Herzegovina) on Operation Lodestar. SFOR had assumed the Implementation Force (IFOR) duties. Again, the regiments deployed with one squadron, the remainder being deployed in Combat Vehicle Reconnaissance (Tracked) – CVR(T) – or infantry roles. And again, Challenger 2 did not have to fire its main armament in anger, finding that its mere presence was more than enough to quell any potential mischief.

Saif Sareea II

Although not a combat deployment, this was meant to show that British forces could still deploy armour. Part of the reason was that Saddam Hussein's regime was still refusing to comply with UN resolutions and the remainder of the Middle East was far from peaceful. The British government decided to run a 22,000-man, two-month exercise – Exercise Saif Sareea II – in the second half of 2001. Given the close military alliance between the United Kingdom and the United States, Saif Sareea II was conducted in Oman, with the troops working closely with the Sultan of Oman's armed forces.

The terrain chosen by the British was so poor that even the Omani army had never considered training there. The 4th Armoured Brigade sent some sixty-six Challenger 2s, with four squadrons from the Royal Dragoon Guards and a fifth from the Queen's Royal Lancers. Omani forces also took part. No extra money was allocated for desert modifications for the exercise because the British government did not see the need. So, in essence, the Challenger 2 that was configured to fight in Europe participated in the exercise with predictable results. Oman is one of the dustiest and driest areas on earth, and with no special sand filters or other theatre-specific equipment, the penny-pinching MoD set the scene for some embarrassing moments for Challenger 2, providing the press with a field day. The tanks were

This KFOR Challenger 2 seems to be in an overwatch position; the loader's MG is swung to his rear so there is probably no immediate threat. It carries the side armour package and rear fuel drums. To provide extra stowage space, some units have cut one end from the fuel drum and made canvas covers for them: no matter how many bins you fit to a tank it will never be enough for a tank crew. (Bullet Proof Models)

A pair of Challenger 2s on operations in Kosovo. They have the full array of the current side armour packs fitted. The nearest tank has it metrological probe in the operating position. (Military-Today.com)

operating in extreme, dusty conditions and the air filters were failing after a day. The dust entered every nook and cranny, and simply showed that in the current configuration the tanks were not fit for desert warfare. As usual the British press screamed that Challenger 2 was a waste of money, that the MoD had bought the wrong tank. A parliamentary committee found nothing wrong with Challenger 2: rather the fault lay with those who provided the funding (the MoD). The results were soon forthcoming and included new filters and side armour skirt extensions that almost reached the ground. It was just as well for Challenger 2 was going to war.

Operation Telic

In 2003 the British government sent one armoured brigade – the 7th – to support the Coalition in the invasion of Iraq. The brigade operated in two armour-heavy groups and two infantry-heavy groups. This order of battle was conceived to fight a mobile battle deep in the enemy's territory

with artillery support from a regiment of thirty-two AS-90 self-propelled guns and MLRS batteries.

The battlegroups with Challenger 2 as their armour support were as follows: The SCOTS DG Battlegroup which was formed from two squadrons of the SCOTS DG, and the Irish Guards with forty-two Challenger 2s and twenty-eight Warriors The 2 RTR (Royal Tank Regiment) Battlegroup was formed from two reinforced 2nd Royal Tank Regiment squadrons with forty-two Challenger 2s and twenty-eight Warriors APCs' from The Light Infantry. The Black Watch Battlegroup was formed from a detached squadron each of 2 RTR and SCOTS DG with twenty-eight Challenger 2s and forty-two Warriors from the Black Watch. Finally, the Royal Regiment of Fusiliers Battlegroup was formed from eighteen Challenger 2s of the Queen's Royal Lancers and forty-two Warriors of the Royal Regiment of Fusiliers. Making up the crews were a large number of reservists including troops from the Royal Wessex Yeomanry,

This Royal Dragoon Guards (RDG) Challenger 2 at speed during Exercise Saif Sareea II, clearly showing the dust problems. Until modifications were rushed into service, vast amounts of dust would be drawn into the air cleaners, totally blocking them. (Wikicommons)

Right: A Challenger 2 on patrol in Iraq, probably during the war or on one of the first Operation Telic missions, as the tanks are still painted in desert colours. The crew are keeping their heads down, trying to gain as much protection as possible from snipers. (Brian Gill, Challenger Tank Appreciation Society)

Below: In this view, the extended dust flaps on the rear wing are shown to good effect. Also visible is the TEC (thermal exhaust cowl) fitted over the exhaust outlet to deflect the hot exhaust gases to reduce the infrared signature. (Plain Military)

Right: This Challenger has stopped while on patrol in the Amarah area. Compare the clutter on the RDG tank to this, and notice that, unusually, it is fitted with the dozer blade kit. (Trevor Gray, Challenger Tank Appreciation Society)

This RDG soldier is wearing the new (at the time) one-piece flameproof desert tank suit, a very useful item of clothing. (Rob Griffin courtesy of RDG)

a TA unit that supplies trained soldiers to support the regular units.

Along with the associated infantry elements, armoured training after Operation Granby had reflected the expectation of fighting another Operation Granby. However, Operation Telic proved to be slightly different and unexpected. All the acclimatization and in-theatre training were completed before the tanks were moved to a camp area codenamed Camp Coyote for upgrading. Up-armouring kits were fitted as well as the special desert modifications introduced following Exercise Saif Sareea II. Also fitted by the engineers from various companies back in the UK was the Garmin GPS. This proved invaluable. As a fitted item it had an external antenna which meant that if the crew were closed down, they still received a signal. This was greatly appreciated by the crews as during Granby many had purchased their own-hand-held GPSs but once closed down they lost the signal. The distinctive side panels on the turret were also fitted, meant as an aid to identification. Another new item was the thermal exhaust cowl (TEC) fitted over the exhaust outlets to carry the exhaust to the rear of the tank. Although it was not thought that the Iraqis had thermal imaging, it was felt better to be safe than sorry. Also available were the bulldozer kits and although some tanks used them to great effect, they were not liked by the crews. The crew also had the new issue flameproof tank suits to wear which were improvements over previous ones. Once all this was done, it was time to fully load the tanks with ammunition, fuel and supplies before a constant stream of briefings to keep the troops abreast of the situation. Then finally it was playing the old soldier's game of waiting.

The waiting finally ended on 21 March 2003 as the British advanced towards their objective of Basra, a day after the air campaign began. The British division advanced about 100 kilometres on the first day – an amazing distance for an armoured unit in enemy-held territory – and met little opposition. The reason for this became plain as the they advanced further. They started to come across Iraqi T-55 and Chinese-copy T-59 tanks, in well-dug-in positions. But the crews had abandoned them and disappeared, with many disposing of their uniforms and returning home. It seemed as if the whole Iraqi National Army had decided to call it a day. However, the British troops were not complacent as they knew that the Fedayeen and the Republican Guard were still willing to fight on.

The role of the Challenger 2 in the offensive switched on the second day from being the armoured spearhead at the head of each mechanized battlegroup to that of infantry support. One of 2 RTR's first heavy contacts with enemy forces in this role took place at Az Zubayr. The original plan called for teams of snipers to take up positions overlooking a Fedayeen headquarters. Unfortunately, the snipers were spotted and their intended targets managed to slip away. The Fedayeen later engaged the tanks and infantry with rocket-propelled grenades (RPGs) and heavy machine-gun fire. The 2 RTR tanks and the Warriors of the accompanying infantry responded with 7.62mm chain-gun fire and 120mm HESH fire before pulling back and taking the sniper team with them. The road to Basra lay open but the decision to surround the city was taken and operations slowed in tempo.

Even with thermal imaging equipment, nocturnal operations are confusing and the risk from friendly fire is much higher than in daylight. In a night-time engagement against Iraqi armoured forces on 25 March 2003, a Challenger 2 belonging to the Queen's Royal Lancers was mistaken for an enemy vehicle. It was fired upon and destroyed by a HESH round fired by a 2 RTR Challenger 2. Details of the inquiry that followed showed that despite provision of IFF (identification friend or foe) panels developed from experience in Desert Storm, and the use of (TOGS) thermal observation and gunnery sight), the QRL Challenger 2 had been mistaken at long distance for an Iraqi MT-LB (an APC) operating in the same area. The HESH strike had freakishly passed through the open commander's cupola hatch, and the tank exploded as it detonated inside the turret. The ammunition inside the tank exploded through sympathetic detonation even though the bag charges were inside armoured bins. The explosion lifted the turret into the air and dropped it onto the engine deck, killing the vehicle commander and driver. The gunner and loader standing outside the tank were badly injured by the explosion.

Unbelievably the armchair experts took this incident to criticize the design of Challenger 2, saying that if the tank had been designed with turret blow-off panels like the Abrams and Leopard 2, this would not have happened. This is a silly argument as these tanks have those panels due to the fact their ammunition is stored in the turret, while Challenger 2's is stored below the turret ring. It was a freak shot and noting more, and rather tasteless to even bring it up so close to the incident.

The battles around Basra raged on, covered by direct media coverage that made much of one engagement that surpassed the fame achieved by a Challenger 1 during Operation Granby. On 29 March 2003, a Challenger 2, commanded by Major Tim Brown of A Squadron SCOTS DG, claimed the longest-range tank-versus-tank kill. The target of one of the armoured raids was a Fedayeen base including one of the communications towers used for propaganda broadcasts by the Ba'ath Party. The tower was knocked out with APFSDS fired by Brown's gunner, Corporal Vince McLeod. The entire engagement was filmed by an embedded BBC team and appeared on live television in Britain.

The tactics employed by Saddam's diehard supporters were very different from those used in Granby. This caused problems for the Coalition forces as each operation had to be carefully planned to avoid causing civilian casualties and also not sustaining casualties themselves. Raids using Challenger 2 were carried out but the enemy proved to be very elusive.

The main threat to armour was the rocket-propelled grenade, a simple, lightweight projectile that can be operated by one man, from well-hidden locations. Every armoured squadron sustained multiple RPG attacks during the battles around Basra. The Challenger 2s of 2 RTR were repeatedly hit by RPG projectiles but none was damaged seriously; the commonest debilitating damage was damaged optics. Fedayeen anti-tank teams were shot down with coaxial machine guns or blown to pieces with HESH. The Challenger's Chobham armour proved its worth in protecting against RPG fire. One tank was recorded to have been hit seventy times without serious damage. As an anti-personnel weapon, 120mm HESH proved lethal at ranges as short as 25 metres. The new CHARM (Challenger Armament) depleted-uranium APFSDS-T ammunition was used against enemy opposition and multiple rounds were fired at enemy strongpoints as well as at pinpoint targets on operations in Iraq.

There were many incidents and many of those involved individual tanks that had been detailed for specific operations. One that really made the news and had the embodiment of the true cavalry sprit was what became known as Operation Dagger. This involved two tanks from the King's Royal Hussars in an operation to rescue some special forces troops who had be captured by the Iraqis and were being held in the jail at Al-Jameat. The plan was for the Challengers to escort the rescue troops on Warrior APCs and who were in the words of Corporal Stew Baird 'a scary looking bunch'. On arrival at the prison, negotiations ensued in an attempt to have the SAS troops released peacefully. These failed so the Challengers took up position. At around midnight the go-go command came over the radio and Baird launched his tank literally at the prison walls. He went in with the gun front, not always a good

This is call sign 20 from the RDG, showing how all the bar armour is located around the turret. The driver's camera can be seen in the centre of the glacis plate. (Courtesy RDG)

Challenger fans having a closer look. This tank exhibits the major upgrades to the hull front, with the solid armour pack on the glacis, and the driver's camera visible in the centre of the glacis. Notice the plastic covers over the fire extinguishers. The turret has the wire cutter, remote weapon station, side armour and bar armour. (QRH)

A close-up of a QRH tank showing to good effect the mounting of the Dorchester armour block, the driver's forward-facing camera and the electronics for dealing with IEDs. (QRH via Challenger Tank Appreciation Society)

idea when breaching walls but he wanted the thickest turret armour in front; it also gave him the opportunity to make use of the tank's weapons if needed. Although he managed to only breach two of the outer walls, it was enough to allow the SAS troops to storm the prison and rescue their comrades. Baird also relates that the SAS

in their normal style used lots of explosives. Images of his tank still covered in rubble were on the front pages of the papers the next day.

Another incident that showed the true value of the add-on armour packs concerned the tank of Captain De Silva of the SCOTS DG. His tank was hit on the lower armour pack on the glacis plate: nothing unusual about that but the 100mm round was fired from what had been classed as an abandoned Iraqi T-55. It hit fair and square in the centre of the ERA (explosive reactive armour) pack, which did what it was designed to do: explode. In so doing, it disrupted the round and prevented penetration. Apart from the shock, the crew were unhurt. There are many more tales like that but these are outside the scope of this book.

Finally, the ceasefire came into force on 8 April 2003, and the war was over. However, the tanks had to remain in theatre to police the country for some time as the whole infrastructure had disintegrated. This meant that the QRL and 2 RTR stayed in the area for several months longer. The continuing presence of foreign troops became a source of considerable discontent to the Iraqis, causing a rise in the number of Iraqis joining the insurgents. These groups were soon creating major problems. The last thing the UK government wanted was to be drawn into a long peacekeeping operation. The type of urban patrolling that this entailed meant the Challenger 2 was being used in an unsuitable environment. All-around protection had to be provided against RPG attack with Chobham armour blocks added to the turret sides and bar armour on the rear of the tank. Bar armour had been designed and fitted to vehicles on occupation duties. It was nothing more than sets of steel slats welded together to form a protective cage around the vehicle. The intention was to trap the warhead of an RPG round and possibly even detonate it before it could hit the the hull or turret. Several vehicles were recorded to have come back from patrols with RPG projectiles stuck between the slats, so it obviously worked.

During this period the suitability of armour protection was constantly looked at. The first to go was the ROMOR ERA. During continuing Operation Telic patrols in August 2006, the driver of a Queen's Royal Hussars Challenger 2, Trooper Sean Chance, lost three of his toes when an RPG-29 tandem warhead round penetrated the ERA protecting the lower bow plate of the hull during an engagement in Amara. The tank had already been hit by ten to fifteen RPGs and was under sniper fire. Despite his injuries, Chance was able to reverse the vehicle to the regimental aid post. This incident caused great concern because the ensuing investigation concluded that the ROMOR ERA panels struck by the RPG had failed to explode. Less than a year later, on

A rear view of an RDG Challenger showing to good effect the layout of the add-on bar armour. Also shown are the two coils of razor wire which can be used to make a very quick vehicle checkpoint, among other applications. (Rob Griffin courtesy of RDG)

6 April 2007 in Basra, a large improvised explosive device (IED) shaped charge detonated underneath a Challenger 2. It penetrated the belly armour, resulting in the driver losing a leg and causing minor injuries to another soldier. The belly plate was a known weak spot on all Western MBTs against large IEDs. To be fair, one can add armour to any area to meet any threat but eventually you end up with a 100-ton behemoth that cannot move. Naturally this point was lost on the British media, who launched another ill-informed sensationalist crusade blaming the MoD for knowing about this weakness and doing nothing. A comprehensive upgrade of the Challenger's frontal armour resulted. The frontal ERA was replaced by a block of Dorchester armour and extra add-on plates were designed to enhance the belly plate armour.

By the time the Royal Dragoon Guards returned to Basra for Operation Telic 11, they found that the Challenger 2s looked very different from when they had last been in theatre during Telic 5. Urban operations had led to many precautions against IED and RPG attacks, with the adoption of new side armour arrays for the hull, and the turret sides fitted with blocks of Dorchester armour in addition to the bar armour described above.

Protection now also extended to electronic countermeasures equipment to combat remote-detonation devices, most visible on the rear of the Challenger's turret roof. The long, flat antenna behind the crew's hatches was nicknamed the 'bird table'. As part of countermeasures to the IED threat, the 'bird table' and its associated antenna jammed electronic signals, coupled with equipment located on the front wings of the tank designed to counter IED's. One extra item on the upgrades was that some vehicles had the loader's periscope removed as seen earlier

This rather atmospheric view is of the RDG tank park during Operation Telic. There is now no attempt to paint the tanks in desert colours, the Barracuda camouflage net being supplied in a variety of colours to aid this task. The wire cutter (just behind the left bank of smoke dischargers) is designed to cut any wires stretched across the route. The tank has also been fitted with the remote weapon station. (Rob Griffin courtesy of RDG)

Challenger 2 powering through the Copehill Down training village, using its on-board smoke generator to create its own smokescreen. (Nick Stearn, Challenger Tank Appreciation Society)

This good side view of an RDG Challenger during Operation Telic shows the mixture of old and new parts as denoted by the different-colour paint; also, the wire cutter is plainly visible by the smoke dischargers. This tank also has the bar armour fitted, a cheap but effective way to negate rocket-propelled grenades. (Rob Griffin courtesy of RDG)

A scene that will be familiar to many: the vast plains of the training area at BATUS in Alberta, Canada. The tanks have their call signs painted on the skirting plates and turrets so that they can be readily identified by the safety staff. The number on the front is known as the 'zap' number, used in the event of having to report an incident, and to determine an individual vehicle. This is necessary as the call-sign system has more than one vehicle using a particular call sign. (Challenger Tank Appreciation Society)

A nice view of the remote weapon station. To the left is the ammunition box with the feed coming out of it into the gun on the left. The exhausted links and cases are allowed to fall onto the turret roof to be cleared later. On the right is the camera and night-viewing equipment. (QRH)

This RDG Challenger shows most of the modifications in use at the time. The glacis plate has a forward-looking camera and on either side is the electronic defensive suite to help protect against IEDs. The name can just be seen on the front of the side armour, a typical cavalry choice. The use of Barracuda camouflage net changes the colour of the tank but even so some original parts are still desert yellow. (Rob Griffin courtesy of RDG)

and the resulting space fitted with a remote weapons station. This unit could be fitted either with .50 Browning or more usually in UK service the well-loved GPMG 7.62mm machine gun. This coupled with its camera and internal controls allowed the loader to provide fire from under armoured cover, ideal for fighting in built-up areas.

Eventually all the Challengers and the rest of the British troops finally left Iraq, leaving it for the Iraqis to rebuild their nation. Challenger 2 had come through the conflict and confounded its critics, who still remained. Its reliability and more importantly its survivability came in for much praise from its crews and from other nations, who were always glad to have Challenger 2 in armoured support.

Once home, the never-ending cycle of training continued, with exercises at British Army Training Unit Suffield in Canada (BATUS) or at home honing urban fighting skills and river crossings. Ranges are also in use constantly to enable the crews to keep their skills up to date or those happy days camping on Salisbury Plain.

Each day on the ranges the ritual known as bore-sighting is performed. It is carried out to ensure that the sights and the gun are aligned. This is done by inserting a special optic into the bore and, with a controller looking through it, he guides the gunner to use his hand controls to lay on the bore-sighting target: they then can adjust the sights. Purists will notice that the operator has his hand on the barrel, a cardinal sin, as it could move the barrel sufficiently to cause an incorrect reading (Courtesy QRH via Trevor Gray)

An RTR Challenger on exercise on Salisbury Plain. The object hanging under the barrel is part of the weapons effect simulator that can be fitted. It allows realistic engagements to be carried out and kills scored. The system uses laser and flash-bang generators, the latest in this type of equipment fitted to tanks; prior to this were Simfire and Simfics, both of which spent most of the lives in the stores as they were awkward to fit and hard to calibrate. (Courtesy RTR via Plain Military)

The first thing you notice about this Challenger 2 is its striking camouflage, the original urban scheme invented by Trooper 'Henry' Wilks of the 4th/7th Royal Dragoon Guards while serving in Berlin. The commanding officer of the Royal Tank Regiment decided to resurrect this scheme and had a troop of his tanks painted in it. (Doug Bradburt, Challenger Tank Appreciation Society)

Operating fully closed down, this Challenger is entering the Copehill Down training village on Salisbury Plain. Fighting in built-up areas is not the most popular of pastimes for tank crews. Hopefully they will have plenty of infantry support to cover them. (Nick Stearn, Challenger Tank Appreciation Society)

This excellent shot shows another way of getting heavy armour across rivers if the bridges have been destroyed. Four M3 bridging rigs have been linked to form a raft and can carry two Challengers at a time. A crossing like this takes a lot of preparation and is fraught with danger. (The Queen's Royal Lancers)

The Future

So, what does 2020 and beyond hold for Challenger 2? The armoured regiments have been decimated and eventually only two Challenger regiments will remain in the British Army, a very sad fact indeed. The MoD seems to be basing its ideas of armour support on the soon-to-be-in-service Ajax, which is based on a 40-year-old hull design that is very large compared to the vehicles it is to replace. It is produced in almost flat-pack design and assembled in Wales. The Warrior is due for upgrade and most think these will be used in lieu of main battle tanks.

The tank-is-dead cry is very active again, but there is nothing today that can produce the shock and awe of the tank in full flow. It can seize ground but will always need infantry support. Those who decry it shout about helicopter gunships and anti-tank missiles. Yes, they are deadly but in fluid battlefields they are not always available. Only time will tell and, who knows, maybe that far-off cavalry bugle will sound the call and once again Challenger 2 will be launched into battle. The MoD has a Challenger 2, unofficially called 'Megatron'. It is always visible at Bovington Tank Fest days, and embodies all the upgrades that could be used on Challenger 2.

So what does the future hold for Challenger 2? Many have already been consigned to the cutting torch, although the MoD claims these are the oldest tanks being disposed of. As this book is being written the Royal Armoured Corps is awaiting the result of the competition that will provide the midlife upgrade to the remaining Challenger 2 fleet. The two main competitors are BAE and the German firm Rheinmetall. This shows the sad fate that has befallen the country that invented the tank: we now have no tank manufacturing capability at all, and some will see it as a bit of a slap in the face for a German firm to be even considered. However, national pride aside, what will we get for our money?

Both contenders will give the tank a life in service till 2035.

BAE have called theirs Black Knight, saying it will remove obsolescence and replace with state-of-the-art new equipment. It offers a new-generation thermal-imaging system with independent sights for the commander and the gunner. It offers a missile-threat system that once it detects incoming missiles, can launch counter-measures. It offers hi-tech front and rear cameras and can detect a threat, automatically training the gun in that direction. BAE makes no mention of rearming the 120mm for a smoothbore.

What then of the German proposal? This is certainly the more radical and, it is suspected, is the one that will be chosen. Firstly, Rheinmetall is designing a brand-new turret to mount their L55 120mm smoothbore gun. This would at last bring it into line with all NATO tank guns and provide commonality of ammunition. The German version does not include an active missile defence system, but if required this could be fitted.

At the moment there is no mention from either company as to upgrading the powerpack, which is something that many hope will happen. One of the criticisms that has been levelled at both designs is that all the add-ons, especially the sights, are far too tall and will suffer from a close high-explosive round. Whether this is true or not, one would hope that things like this have been taken into account when the designs are being formulated. Whichever design is chosen and how many remaining Challenger 2s are actually modified due to costs, remains to be seen. The result of which company is selected is due to be announced at the end of October 2019. What comes next? Will we buy from a foreign nation? When Challenger retires, will tanks at last be redundant? Meanwhile, Challenger 2 is poised, ready for whatever is thrown at it next.

Not a drop of dirt to be seen: one of RTR's Challengers freshly painted in the urban scheme. It does look slightly out of place on Salisbury Plain, but once it moves into the specialist village known as Copehill Down, then the scheme comes into its own. A good project for modelling, like the larger R/C Challenger models it is not an easy scheme to apply. (Jake Foster, Challenger Tank Appreciation Society)